A Monarch Americana Book

THE DILLINGER STORY

Here Is The Dramatic Story Of
John Dillinger—Gangster, Bank Robber,
Killer and Public Enemy

Ovid Demaris

Author of Lucky Luciano

MONARCH BOOKS, INC.

Derby, Connecticut

THE DILLINGER STORY

A Monarch Americana Book

Published in July, 1961

Copyright © 1961 by Ovid Demaris

Photographs from Wide World

Monarch Books are published by MONARCH BOOKS, INC., Capital Building, Derby, Connecticut, and represent the works of outstanding novelists and writers of non-fiction especially chosen for their literary merit and reading entertainment.

Printed in the United States of America

CHAPTER ONE

The rain swept across Lake Michigan in cold gray sheets that morning, crashing against the prison wall with the impact of a tidal wave. Inside the main gatehouse, John Dillinger waited, his face pressed against the bulletproof glass, his yellow slate eyes carefully observing every movement along the wet street.

Behind him two heavily armed uniformed guards spoke in hushed tones. He could see them reflected in the thick glass. And he could see the gunrack with the submachine guns, rifles and riot guns. Hanging from wall hooks, next to the artillery, were four bulletproof steel vests.

A moment later a black sedan pulled up at the curb and stopped. Dillinger spun around, raising the collar of his thin coat, pulling down the snap brim of his soft hat.

"Open them gates," he said. "I'm coming out."

He came through the opened gate running lightly on tiptoes, skipping around puddles, the parole paper clutched tightly in his fist. The car door flew open and he ducked inside. Water dripped from his hat, down his pale face and into his opened, laughing mouth.

"Homer, you old son-of-a-bitch," he cried, clasping the driver's hand in a firm handshake.

Homer Van Meter was also laughing. "Johnnie,, Johnnie, Johnnie," he chanted. "You look great."

"I feel great," Dillinger said. "Gimme a butt."

Homer handed him a new pack. "Want a drink, Johnnie? Got a pint of bonded stuff in the glove compartment."

"Let's get this jalopy rolling," he said, lighting the cigarette. "The quicker I'm out of here, the better I'm gonna like it."

Homer jammed the stick into first and roared away,

5

grinding the gears in his eagerness to demonstrate the powerful take-off.

Dillinger took a stiff pull on the pint before settling back in the seat. "Where'd you get the jalopy?"

"Bought it," Homer said, staring myopically through the blurred windshield. "Paid cold cash for it. How you like it, Johnnie?"

"Got the new V-8 engine?"

"Yeah. It'll clock ninety."

"Been reading about it," Dillinger said. "Where d'you get the dough?"

Homer giggled. "A nice little bank in Kansas."

"Read about that, too. Didn't know you was in on it."

"I was the wheelman."

Dillinger nodded and took another pull on the bottle. "Who you working with?"

"Eddie Bentz," Homer said proudly.

Dillinger raised his eyebrows. "Thought he was dead."

"Hell, no," Homer said. "Eddie's been at it twenty-five years. Biggest in the business."

Dillinger puffed on the cigarette and stared out across the rain-swept street. "Crummy day," he said. They were driving through the business district of Michigan City. "Been here nine years and this is my first look at this burg. Crummy."

"What're you down in the mouth for?" Homer asked.

"Hell, this is graduation day. Tonight it's wine, women and thick juicy steaks." He giggled. "The day I got out I got drunk as a hoot owl. Passed out in a whorehouse in Chicago. Boy, I made up for seven years in seven days. That's where I met Marie."

"Marie?"

"Yeah, Marie Conforti. Johnnie, that broad's got everything."

"Where is she?"

"Waiting for us in Chicago. Got me a nice little place on Halsted Street. Been shacking it ever since that first night."

"Fix me up," Dillinger said.

"Hey, Johnnie—"

6

"She's a whore, ain't she?"

"No more. I straightened her out."

Dillinger gave a harsh laugh. "You straightened her out, Homer."

"Sure, why not?"

Dillinger shook his head, amused at the idea. Homer Van Meter measured barely five feet. He was a skinny little runt with a large head, a long hooked nose, and a pointed chin. His eyes, which were a washed-out blue, stared moistly out from deep sockets with a perpetual look of harassment. "You don't look like no lady's man to me, pal."

Homer squirmed uneasily, his neck reddening. "Aw, come on, Johnnie. Lay off. This dame's crazy about me."

Dillinger turned on the seat. "Tell me about her. What does she look like naked?"

Homer giggled. "Stacked."

"Big chest?"

"You bet."

"That's what I like," he said, his voice soft and suggestive. "I thought about it a lot in stir. Fix me up with her for tonight."

Homer's jaw dropped, his animal-like eyes darting with panic. "Aw, come on, Johnnie. Marie's my gal—"

Dillinger's hard knuckles smashed into Homer's mouth, his lascivious purr turning into a snarl. "You forgetting who's boss, Homer?"

The car swerved—Homer got it under control. "It ain't that, Johnnie," he whined, "and I know how you must feel after nine years in stir but—okay, you can have her tonight. It'll be okay. She's great."

They drove in silence for a while.

"My wife was great," Dillinger said, closing his eyes.

"You never told me you was married, Johnnie."

Dillinger's eyes remained closed and there was a strange softness in his voice when he spoke. "She was just a kid. Sixteen. I remember how beautiful and sweet-smelling she was. All I got to do is close my eyes and I can see her just like she was then. She had a build like one of them Greek statues."

7

"Was she a blonde?"

Dillinger opened his eyes, startled by the question. "I don't know," he said. "I can't remember her face."

"Then how you know she was beautiful?"

He shook his head, puzzled. "Funny," he said. "All them years, night after night, I dreamed about her. Sometimes she was stark naked and other times all dressed up." He paused and chain-lit another cigarette. "But it didn't matter, I could always see how beautiful she was."

"You going back to her?"

"Naw. She divorced me five years ago and married some crum in Mooresville."

The torrential downpour had eased to a light sprinkle by the time they arrived in Chicago. Dillinger smiled happily at the crowded streets, the nearly empty pint bottle in his hand.

"This is my kind of town," he said, shaking the bottle.

"Great town. Lots of action."

"Look at me," Dillinger said. "I'm twenty-nine years old. Gonna be thirty next month. You know something? I've been in this burg only once in my whole life. And then I was on the lam."

Homer sneered wisely. "How do you like that booze, Johnnie?"

"Okay. Pretty weak but okay. Better than that poison in stir. That stuff blows holes right through your guts." He laughed, spreading his arms wide. "Look at 'em, Homer. People. Thousands of free people. I'm out of that crummy pen." He paused, the laughter dying in his throat. "It's like a dream or something. Nine goddamn lousy years down the drain."

"You're lucky," Homer said. "They could have kept you there thirty."

"Yeah. Thirty years. The book. And I was just a kid. My Old Man says, 'plead guilty and they'll go easy on you.' Easy, hell."

"That crummy judge."

"I could kill him."

"Forget it," Homer said. "We're here to celebrate."

8

"Yeah. Where's this Marie?"

"Ready and waiting."

"I'm gonna bust her wide open. Come on, take a swig."

Homer took the bottle and nipped lightly. "You go easy on Marie," he said. "No rough stuff."

Dillinger's yellow eyes hardened. "Don't tell me what to do. Nobody tells me what to do. I'm John Dillinger. I do what I goddamn want to, when I goddamn want to. I'll bust her wide open any time I feel like it. Understand?"

"Take it easy, Johnnie."

"You just shut that fish mouth of yours."

"Sorry, Johnnie."

"You know something? You got a mouth like a fish. You look like you're sucking air all the time. You ugly bastard. That Marie must be a pig to shack up with you. You stink."

"Ah, Johnnie, you're drunk. You don't mean—"

The hard knuckles smashed across his mouth, knocking his head sideways. Homer yelped, twisted the steering wheel, barely missing a truck. A think stream of blood coursed down his chin, falling in tiny drops on his raincoat. There was a hurt look in Homer's moist blue eyes when he turned toward Dillinger.

"You keep forgetting who's boss, Homer. Remember in stir? What I said, went."

Homer nodded meekly.

"Well, I'm still boss. And don't you ever forget it."

"I won't, Johnnie."

"Here, have a drink."

Homer took another small nip and Dillinger killed the bottle. They were friends again. Homer giggled hysterically when Dillinger flung the bottle out of the car window. They were driving through the slums of West Madison, with its pushcarts, hock shops and greasy spoons, and the filth and stench of countless generations of tenement dwellers.

"Look at them slobs," Dillinger said. "Rotting in their own stinking juice. Dumb bastards."

"You think this is something? You oughta see some of the stuff around the stockyards. Them cows live better than people. They've got a shanty town over there that

9

goes for miles. Made out of boxes and tar paper. Makes this place look like the Ritz."

Dillinger shrugged. "Who cares. Let's get to Marie."

There was a furtive, simian wariness in Marie's black, opaque eyes as she studied Dillinger from across the bedroom. She lay on the rumpled bed, clad only in a pair of sheer black step-ins, humorously appliquéd with a pink hand. Her small body was as brown as a coffee bean and her tiny breasts were as hard as walnuts.

"What's the matter, sport? Ain't you satisfied yet?"

"You don't do nothing for me," he said. "With or without them pants."

"They're cute," she said. "Everybody's wearing 'em. It's the latest rage."

"Not where I come from."

She laughed and it sounded like a nervous cough. "I'll bet those sports would pay plenty for what I just gave you for nothing. I'll bet I'd do something for them."

Dillinger loosened his belt and shoved his shirt inside his pants. "Fix me up with somebody."

She grinned slyly. "Want somebody with big ones, sport?"

"Anybody would be bigger than you."

She shrugged and raised her painted eyebrows. "You queer that way, sport?"

"Yeah," he said. "I'm queer that way. And you're gonna be queer some other way if you don't watch that mouth."

She sat up and carefully patted her bobbed hair into place. "My, ain't we tough today."

Dillinger picked up his tie and began to knot it, watching her in the mirror. "Ask Homer," he said. "He'll fill you in on the details."

She stood up and walked to the mirror, standing in front of him, her hands pressing against her hips. "Lots of men like me real fine. I used to be Ana's favorite."

"Cut the advertising. I've already tested the goods."

"I could learn to hate you," she said. "It would be real easy."

10

"Are you or ain't you gonna fix me up?"

"Sure, sport. Evelyn is gonna be here around ten."

His yellow eyes hardened. "Why didn't you tell me that before?"

She shrugged, slowly passing her hands over her hard breasts. "I wanted to take a crack at you myself. You looked cute."

"What time is it?"

"Simmer down, sport. It's only six o'clock."

Dillinger crossed the room and opened the door. "Homer, let's go get that steak."

Homer jumped up from the sofa and rushed into the bedroom, his moist eyes nervously appraising Marie. "Okay, Johnnie. Listen, can I talk to Marie a minute?"

"I'm hungry."

"But, Johnnie. Just two minutes."

"Lay off," Marie cried. "I'm tired."

"Baby, for me, please."

"Let's go," Dillinger said. "I told you I was hungry."

"But Marie's got to dress."

"I ain't got time to wait." He started across the living room and Homer ran after him. Marie's curses followed them all the way down the stairs.

Dinner in a restaurant off the Loop consisted of thick T-bone steaks and French fried potatoes. They drank bonded whiskey from thick coffee mugs.

After a half dozen drinks Dillinger had recaptured the glow he had enjoyed earlier in the afternoon. His eyes sparkled as he gazed about the room, taking in the rich walnut paneling, the red leather upholstered booths, the white-jacketed waiters and the well-dressed patrons.

"Who says there's a depression going on?" he said, grinning knowingly at Homer. "What's a depression anyway? You either got dough or you don't. My Old Man's been in a depression all his goddamn life. You know, like some guys have it rich all their lives. Some have it and some don't. I'm gonna have it."

"You bet," Homer said, pulling out a thick wad of bills from his pocket. Giggling, he bounced it on the table,

11

catching it in midair. "Five minutes' work, Johnnie. That's all. Five minutes and I had five grand in my pocket. See that waiter there? He works five years for this little wad."

Dillinger nodded. "I've got it all figured out. All I need is an organization. Some good boys. Boys with guts and brains like Jack Hamilton and Harry Pierpont."

"Don't forget Charlie Makley and Russell Clark."

Dillinger leaned forward and lowered his voice. "It's all set up," he said. "I'm gonna spring 'em."

Homer sat up straight, his eyes bulging and wet as he looked about him. "When, Johnnie? How you gonna pull that off?"

"We need some dough and artillery first. The details are all worked out. It's gonna go off like clockwork."

"How many guys coming out?"

"Ten. Four of 'em are coming along with me. The other six are on their own."

"I'll help you," Homer said. "Boy, what a gang we'll make. Six guys. We'll knock over Fort Knox. Hey, we get ourselves some choppers. Look out!" He growled, imitating the staccato bark of a submachine gun, waving both index fingers, thumbs up, across the dining room, spraying imaginary bullets into everybody within sight. "Mow 'em down. Kakaboom!"

"And I know just where to get 'em," Dillinger said, grinning.

"Hey, listen," Homer said. "Marie knows lots of important people."

"What are you talking about?"

"Well, she knows Louis Piquett."

"Who's he?"

"He's a mouthpiece for the Capone mob. Used to be the city prosecutor in this town. Big man."

"How'd she get to know him?"

Homer shrugged. "Used to take care of him regular when she worked for Ana Sage."

"I don't need no mouthpiece," he said. "I ain't going to court or jail no more."

"You need contacts," Homer said. "They cool the heat for you."

12

"Okay. When I need 'em, I'll get 'em. First, I've gotta report to that parole screw in Indianapolis and then I'm going home."

"Home?"

Dillinger nodded. "I've got some business to tend to. I'll be back."

They arrived back at the apartment a few minutes before ten. Marie lay sprawled on the sofa, still naked except for her step-ins, dead drunk. Dillinger sat in a chair facing the door and nervously chained-smoked, trying to ignore Homer who lay on the sofa necking with Marie. He waited until eleven o'clock before giving up and stomping off to bed.

The rain had started again, and he lay on his side, listening to its rhythmic tapping on the window panes, narrowing his eyes until the wooden frame looked like steel bars. He had spent more than three thousand nights looking out at bars, and now that he didn't have to look at them, he saw them anyway.

CHAPTER TWO

Mooresville was typical of a hundred other Indiana farm towns in 1933. It had the same dusty, rutted streets; the same sagging, weathered sidewalk planking; and the same aggregation of shabby shops and austere churches.

The only significant difference was Plato's Pool Palace. Owned by a thick-necked, hard-eyed Greek, the Palace catered to a wide variety of vices. A man could shoot pool, drink corn whiskey, play stud poker or look at French postcards.

The front door of the Palace opened at noon and closed at midnight. The back door was opened to drinkers and gamblers till dawn.

John Dillinger had spent his youth in the Palace. By

the time he was seventeen he was a pool shark, playing for the house. Later he became a *raker* in the card games, raking off the house's cut from each pot. The job required ingenuity. Since the Greek was not a trusting soul, each *raker* had to devise his own foolproof system of cheating the house.

Though he handled the cash register in the front part of the Palace, next to the candy counter, the Greek made frequent unscheduled appearances in the back room, always in the hope of catching his *raker* secreting part of the take. Capture meant more than just losing a job. It meant permanent banishment. A punishment worse than death in a one-pool-parlor town.

Dillinger arrived in Mooresville late the next afternoon. He cruised leisurely through town in Homer's new Ford V-8, dressed in the latest underworld Chicago fashion: pinstriped black suit, black shirt, white tie, black homburg hat, and pearl gray spats over black patent leather shoes. In his wallet were new crisp bills totaling five hundred dollars.

His father's farm was three miles west of town. The Old Man was out in the unpainted lean-to which served as a barn for two milk cows and one tired old plough horse. The house was also unpainted, a two-story frame house without architectural ancestors. Chickens ran and cackled across the front yard, pecking away at the trunks of the huge box elders and cottonwoods. Dillinger sped up the dirt driveway, narrowly missing a bleating nanny goat, and brought the car to a dusty halt beside the front porch.

Moments later John Dillinger, Sr. came out of the barn and ambled slowly toward the car. He was an old man, sharp-featured and bone-thin. He wore bib coveralls and a black stocking cap pulled down over his ears. His nose was red and the nostrils glistened moistly.

Dillinger stepped out of the Ford and waited beside the opened car door, one hand resting on the window sill, the other in his pocket.

The old man nodded in recognition. "Howdy, son," he said. His voice was splinter-dry.

14

"Hi," Dillinger said. "How you been, Pa?"

"Fair to middling. And yourself?"

"No complaint."

"That's your automobile?"

"Yeah."

"Mighty fine looking automobile. Must have cost a lot of money."

"It's the latest model."

The old man nodded. "Nice suit of clothes. They give you that at the prison?"

Dillinger laughed. "Pa, they give you nothing at the prison. Just a lot of hard time."

"That's what I reckoned."

"How's sis?"

"Fine."

"Her man working?"

"Yep."

Dillinger played with the coins in his pocket for a while. "What you gonna plant this year?"

The old man turned to gaze at the twenty acres of barren land, nodding his head. "Potatoes, I reckon. Not much else worth planting nowadays."

"I suppose not."

"Raised potatoes last year," he said, still nodding. "Had to plough 'em under. Couldn't sell 'em nohow. Wouldn't bring a dime a gunny sack."

"So why plant 'em this year?"

"Well," the old man said, raising his stocking cap to scratch the back of his head. "Figure other folks won't be fool enough to grow 'em this year after what happened last year and all."

"Maybe, you're all gonna be fools."

"Don't reckon so," he said, wiping his nose with his index finger. "Got hurt real bad last year. Figure they're gonna be mighty skitterish this year. Besides, I've got a cellar full of seed spuds."

Dillinger moved away from the car, toward the house. "Got anything to eat?"

"Got some eggs and milk."

15

"That figures," he said, quickening his step. The old man ambled after him, wiping his nose and scratching his head.

The kitchen was the largest room in the house, and the most imposing piece of furniture in it was a huge, circular oak table, covered by a cracked oilcloth. Only three of the original set of eight chairs remained. There was an old iron wood stove with a wood box and coal bucket nearby, a lead sink, a linoleum-covered counter top, a washstand with a gray enameled washpan, a slop bucket, a galvanized water bucket and dipper, a leather strop, a rocking chair with a padded, flowered chintz cover, an oval mirror adorned by ruffled oilcloth and curtain-covered cupboards. The only wall decoration was an enormous calendar of a young girl in a large sunbonnet standing awkwardly in a field of daisies. Underneath the picture, in large black type, was the name of the local feed store. Except for the year on the calendar nothing had changed.

Johnnie plunked himself into the rocking chair. The old man had changed. He looked a hundred years older.

"Want me to fix you something?" his father asked, walking to the cupboard.

"Yeah. Scrambled eggs. Got some coffee?"

The old man nodded. "How about some home fries?"

"Fine. Fix anything you've got. I'm real hungry."

"I'll have a little something myself. The older I get the more I eat, it seems. Got the worse god-awful appetite. Hungry all the time, I reckon."

Johnnie smoked and rocked while the old man prepared the food. "Heard about Lizzie," he said. "Thinking of marrying again?"

The old man smiled. "Nope. Two women is enough for a man. Lizzie was a good woman. Took good care of you when your own mother died. Treated you like one of her own kin. You was only a little shaver then—no more than three or four. Can't recollect exactly."

"What she die of?"

"Heart. One day she was healthy as a horse and the next she was gone. Makes a man think."

"We all have to go sometime," Dillinger said, unable

16

to feel any emotion for his dead stepmother. She had always seemed like a visitor in his father's house—someone who had just dropped in to sit a spell, to stare out silently into space, her plain, lined face expressionless. She had just been Old Lizzie, who did the chores and kept out of everybody's way. What his own mother had been like, he didn't know. His father never spoke of her. Once there had been a tintype of her on the wall in his father's room, and he had stared at it, wondering about the straight, thin mouth and the large, liquid eyes and the soft, brown hair coiled in a chignon on the nape of a swanlike neck. He had been very young then, and still intrigued by the unknown quality of the woman who stared down at him without love or recognition. When asked, his father had replied automatically, "She was a good woman." The next day, the tintype had disappeared, never to return. The image in his mind had also disappeared, as quickly and as permanently.

"Yep, I reckon so. My turn is coming. I feel poorly in the mornings." He turned from the stove with the skillet in one hand and the coffee pot in the other. "Come and get it," he said. "Reckon it's as ready as it's ever gonna be."

They ate in silence at first, both men wolfing down their food with slugs of hot coffee.

"Been a hard winter," the old man said.

"So I noticed," Johnnie said. "Ain't started to plough yet?"

"Ground frozen solid. Thaw was real late this year."

"You wasn't waiting for me, was you?"

The old man toyed with his eggs. "I'm getting old," he said. "Them fellas at the state capital gave you that parole so you could help me. I got all the people around here to sign a petition as to how I was getting old and needed you to help me."

"Yeah," Johnnie said. "That's what the parole screw told me this morning. Seems you went all the way up to the governor."

"Yep. He signed it himself. It took a lot of doing."

"I'm not gonna help you," Johnnie said. "I'm not gonna be no dirt farmer."

The old man removed his stocking cap and scratched

17

his head with both hands. "I need you, son. My back and arms ain't what they used to be. I'm gonna be seventy-three come next birthday."

"I ain't what I used to be either," Dillinger said.

"That's what I was hoping," the old man said, replacing the cap on his head, pulling it back down over his ears.

"Pa, I'm just gonna stay here a couple of hours. I've got people waiting for me in Chicago."

The old man stared at him with blank eyes.

"See that car out there? See these clothes? Well, you don't get things like that dirt farming. You get nothing dirt farming. Nothing but a broken back and an early grave. I ain't never done it and I ain't gonna start now—not even for the parole board."

"I didn't really think you would," the old man said. "You ain't never gonna change. You got your head full of fancy ideas and nothing but trouble is gonna come of it."

Johnnie pushed back his plate and stood up. "No sense arguing about it," he said. "My mind's made up."

"What's that parole officer in Indianapolis gonna say about it?"

"Screw him," Johnnie said. "He ain't never gonna see me again."

"Son, you break your parole and they'll have you back in prison in no time flat. I'm giving you a chance to work hard and make up for the wrong you done. Farming is a good life. You find yourself a good woman and settle down. Someday this here farm will be yours."

Johnnie shook his head. "How dumb can you get?" he queried. "This farm ain't worth the powder to blow it to hell. It ain't never been nothing but a pile of horse manure.

"The land is good, son. When good times come again, a hard-working man can do right well for himself farming this here land."

"Good-bye," Johnnie said. "And thanks for the grub."

"Ain't you gonna sit a spell?"

"I've been sitting for nine years," Dillinger answered. "I ain't got no time to sit no more."

The old man remained at the table, his bleak eyes moist

18

as he stared fixedly at his son. "I tried to help you, son. I worked hard to get you out of prison. I need you."

"I'm going, Pa. I don't want to talk about it. I listened to you once and look what it got me. I ain't listening no more to your preaching. Singleton pleaded not guilty and got two years and I got the book. That's all you did for me. And I ain't forgetting it."

"I'm right sorry about that," the old man said. "You did something bad and you had to pay for it."

"What was bad? Stealing the money or getting caught?"

"Stealing is against the laws of man and God. I taught you the right way when you was small."

"You taught me to be poor," he said. "That's all. Poor white trash."

"Son, I provided—"

"The hell with it," Dillinger shouted. "I'm going. You just sit here and rot in your crummy hole. Not me."

The old man stood up, realizing that it was impossible to hold him any longer. He limped across the room, massaging his arthritic legs as he walked. "Are you gonna visit your sister?"

"I don't have time."

The old man bit his lower lip, tears suddenly brimming at the corners of his faded blue eyes. "Good-bye, son," he said, offering him his thin calloused hand. "Take care of yourself."

"Yeah, sure," Dillinger said, giving the hand a quick shake. "I'll be in touch with you."

"What if that parole officer comes nosing around?"

Dillinger laughed. "Tell him to drop dead."

It was dark when he returned to Mooresville. He parked in front of the pool parlor and sat in the car, smoking. Through the dirty plate glass window he could see that four of the six tables were in use.

A young man stood behind the candy counter, drinking a bottle of soda pop and gnawing on a candy bar. The Greek didn't seem to be anywhere about. There was a gang of young punks around the pinball machine, most of them in high school football sweaters.

19

Archie, the town drunk, sat on the long bench which ran the entire length of the room, his shoulders hunched over, his dirty plaid cap pulled down over his eyebrows. Archie had been a drunk for as long as Dillinger could remember; drank everything from bay rum to sterno. Once while he had been in the john he had seen Archie straining a can of sterno through an old dirty handkerchief.

Spellbound, he had watched him gulp down the oily liquid, his whole face changing like that Dr. Jekyll in the movie. His body had stiffened, every nerve vibrating, his eyes bugging out of his emaciated face, his hands and legs clasped rigidly around the huge water pipe behind the toilet. He had coughed and wheezed, the tears streaming down his gray, corrugated cheeks. The spasm had lasted minutes. Afterwards he had seemed like a new man. Winking at him, he had walked out jauntily, a big sly smile on his ravaged face.

There were a lot of things John Dillinger could have remembered that night. The years in Indianapolis when he played first base on the high school team. Saturdays when he worked in his father's grocery store. Sunday school at the Quaker church. The band concerts and picnics. All the things that had occupied his life from the age of three to sixteen while he lived in the slums of the big city. Then back to Mooresville and the farm.

Falling in love with a young high school girl who lived on the right side of the tracks, and then her Old Man busting it up. Joining the Navy in a fit of depression, only to desert six months later while on leave in Boston. He had come back home and his father had fixed everything, even to an honorable discharge. At the age of twenty he had married Beryl Hovis, a sixteen-year-old schoolgirl. He had gone back to the pool parlor, spending his days and nights there, while Beryl waited for him at his father's farm.

Beryl had really loved him. That was one thing he was sure of. She had never complained about the late hours at the poolroom. She had understood that it was his job. He earned more money in one week at the poolroom than farm hands earned in a month. He took her to the movies occasionally, and sometimes to a barn dance. She was the

20

prettiest thing he had ever seen and he liked showing her off to the guys. Sometimes, in the afternoon, she came into town with the old man, and would wait outside the poolroom until somebody saw her and fetched him from the back room. He brought her in once and let her play the pinball machine and all the guys' tongues were hanging out when she left. Later they kidded about it, and he told them she was a wildcat in bed. He saw the envy in their eyes and it gave him a good feeling deep inside.

And then there had been the Greek. All his troubles had started on the night he was caught stashing away a fin in his hatband. The Greek had raised holy hell, striking him in the face and kicking at him while he ran around the pool tables, pleading for the Greek to listen to him. But the Greek hadn't listened.

"Get out," he had shrieked. "Get out and stay out, you crook, you gangster, you highway robber."

Everybody had laughed at him. Only Ed Singleton had not laughed. He had followed Johnnie outside, patting him on the back, consoling him by cursing the Greek. They had gone into the alley behind the Palace and had sat there, drinking corn and talking.

Singleton, already a two-time loser, enjoyed the reputation of a tough guy. "Forget him, Johnnie. Want to get your hands on some real dough? I'll show you how."

"How much?" he asked, taking another drink.

"At least five hundred. This guy carries a wad on him big enough to choke a horse. You can see it bulging out of his back pocket."

"Who is it?"

Singleton grinned, his head nodding. "B. F. Morgan," he said.

"The grocer?"

"Now, listen, Johnnie. I'll tell you what to do. Don't worry about nothin'."

An hour later they waited behind a tree in front of the grocer's house at the edge of town. "That's him," Singleton said. "Now don't forget. Just walk up to him and slug him. I'll frisk him."

Dillinger stepped out from behind the tree, a length

of lead pipe held high over his head. "Gimme your dough," he said.

Startled, Morgan jumped back. "What do you think you're doin'?" he asked in a trembling voice.

"Give me your dough and I won't hurt you," Dillinger said, slowly advancing on the grocer.

"You leave me be," Morgan warned. "I ain't got no money."

"You're a liar," Dillinger·shouted, swinging down with the pipe. It smashed into the grocer's forehead with blinding force. He staggered to his knees, his arms reaching out for the pipe. Then, gasping loudly, he doubled over, collapsing on his face, unconscious.

Singleton was on top of him in an instant, rolling him over, his hands deftly searching his pockets. "Here it is, Johnnie," he cried, holding up the thick elastic-bound roll of bills for his inspection. "Let's get out of here."

Later when they counted the take it amounted to over five hundred dollars. They split it down the middle and drove to Chicago in Singleton's old Star. They were drunk for a week; and then, broke again, they drove back to Mooresville, where the police anxiously awaited their return.

Following his father's advice, Dillinger did not secure legal counsel. Instead, he entered a plea of guilty and threw himself on the mercy of the court. The court felt no mercy. The sentence was the maximum possible under the law for a first offender. Two to twelve years for armed robbery and ten to twenty for conspiracy. In all it had cost him nine years. The most important nine years of his life.

Now seated in the car, a cigarette dangling from his mouth, Dillinger thought of Singleton, remembering his warning about copping a plea. "You're stupid, kid. Never cop a plea. You get the wrong judge and he'll lock you up and throw away the key." Singleton had soon proved the sagacity of his advice. Accompanied by a criminal lawyer. the hardened felon had brazenly walked into court and entered a plea of not guilty. A week later he was found guilty by a jury and promptly sentenced to two years in the federal penitentiary at Michigan City. A year later he was back out on the street.

22

Justice was not only blind, Dillinger thought, his yellow eyes fixed on the dirty plate glass window of the pool parlor, but deaf and dumb as well. Guys in stir were always griping about the raw deals they got. Sure, some of them were putting it on, but a lot of it was straight. There was one thing to be learned from all this. If you were going to do something, do it big—and then fight like hell. Don't be a punk. Be a big man. If you were big enough, you could get away with anything. Even murder.

CHAPTER THREE

Eddie Bentz stood before the large picture window, gazing down at the lights shimmering on the choppy surface of the lake below him, his broad-shouldered back silhouetted against the night sky. Bentz was a big man, well over six feet, with a large head covered with thick, unruly red hair.

"Gentlemen," he said, turning from the window to face the two men on the sofa. "Look at me and tell me what you see."

Bentz was smiling, a long ebony cigarette holder in one hand and a fragile glass of sherry in the other.

"Class," Homer Van Meter said.

Bentz's sharp blue eyes looked pleased by the answer.

"And you, Johnnie? What do you see?"

Dillinger shrugged. "Money. Plenty of money."

"You're both right, gentlemen. You need the one to get the other. They are synonymous. If you remember that, you'll be successful. It takes more than a gun to rob a bank. It takes brains, planning and organization."

Smiling with all the warmth of a gracious host, Bentz sat down in a scarlet wing-back chair, facing the sofa. "Bank robbers are the aristocracy of the criminal profession," he said. "It wasn't always that way. When I started out many years ago, a yegg had to know all about souping

23

or dynamiting safes and vaults. We used to rob in the night then. But the manufacturers of safes got wise and it became more difficult to pour the soup or force the combination knob from its socket.

"Then the automobile came into general use and escape on horseback or by pumping a handcar a few miles down a railroad track became outmoded. So the next thing was daytime robberies. Walk into a bank with a gun and take what you want and get out fast.

"But there was more to it than that. You needed a finger man. You know, someone either on the inside, or at least acquainted with the bank's operation. You had to know how much cash and securities were on hand, and the complete layout—alarms, guards, number of employees, the cops on the beat. Then, of course, you needed a getaway chart."

Dillinger shook his head, squinting his yellow eyes in annoyance.

"I know," Bentz said. "Details. But they're all important in this business if you want to stay alive long enough to spend the swag."

"There are easier ways," Dillinger said.

"Like for instance?"

"Like going in and taking what's in the vault and getting out."

Bentz smiled tolerantly. "That's exactly what I'm trying to tell you, Johnnie. The question is *where* you go in. You shouldn't take the risk without being sure of a just reward." He paused to take a delicate sip of the imported wine. "Let me put it this way, Johnnie. I've been in this business twenty-five years. And in that time, I've never earned less than a hundred thousand a year. That's net. Add it up and you'll see what I mean."

Dillinger nodded, remembering one story he had heard about Bentz in prison. Bentz had masterminded the fabulous one-million-dollar robbery of the Lincoln National Bank and Trust in Lincoln, Nebraska. The way the story went, Bentz had swung into the bank, wearing overalls, jumper, a big straw hat, and a chopper in his mitts.

"How many banks have you robbed?" Dillinger asked.

Bentz scratched his red curly hair with a thick freckled hand. "Don't rightly remember," he said. "Between fifty and a hundred. Look at it this way. You heisted a guy, got five hundred dollars and served nine years in the pen. Not so good. But take me. I heisted all those banks, and I can't remember the number of burglaries, con games, impersonations, grand thefts, plus a couple of snatch jobs. I've served, in my entire lifetime, a total of seven years. You figure it out, Johnnie. Luck?"

He waited for a reaction which didn't come. Then he added, "No, Johnnie. Brains. See, I'm a big, farmerish-looking fellow, sort of easygoing, like to laugh and talk and be chummy with people. That doesn't match up with their ideas about criminals. And I always liked nice things. Went to good shows, stayed at the good hotels, ate at the best places, and was always quiet and gentlemanly about it. People think crooks hide in cellars."

"I don't have time for that junk," Dillinger said.

"Wait a minute. When I'm nice to ordinary people, I'm being selfish. I figure it helps in keeping clear of the law. Why, lots of times people I've known, nice decent people, have warned me that the police had been around asking questions. They figured that a nice, quiet fellow like me couldn't possibly be mixed up in anything crooked, and they wanted to do me a good turn."

"I don't get it," Dillinger said. "Why tell me all this junk, anyway?"

"Simple, my fried. Homer told me of your plans to go into the profession. I work as a caser and adviser for many gangs. I layout the whole job for them, including the getaway chart."

"How much?"

"Not a red penny. You keep all the cash. Give me the stocks and bonds, all the securities."

"Yeah, sure. So you pick jobs with plenty of securities on hand and no cash."

Bentz's blue eyes looked shocked. He stood up, his massive chest swelling as he breathed deeply. "Who are you?" he said, waving the ebony holder before Dillinger's face. "I never heard of you. Some punk kid who gets nine years for pulling a two-bit heist. Who needs you? Let me tell you something, Johnnie. I can pick up that phone right now and call fifty, no a hundred, top men and have them here within twenty-four hours. Eddie Bentz is not just a bank robber. He's a legend." Bentz flipped ashes on the rug and went back to his chair.

"So, okay. You don't need me."

"New business is always welcome."

"How about artillery?"

"I can get guns, vests, soup, anything."

"How much?" Dillinger demanded curtly.

Bentz smiled. "Since you don't care for securities, I'll take ten per cent of the swag on the first° three jobs I line up. Need any men?"

Dillinger stood up. "No thanks," he said. "I'll case my own jobs and get my own artillery.

Bentz shrugged. "Have it your way, Johnnie. But remember, I've had the biggest names in the profession working for me. Alvin Karpis, Ma Barker and her boys, Machinegun Kelly, Pretty Boy Floyd, Verne Miller, Harvey Bailey, Baby Face Nelson. You name him—I've had him."

"John Dillinger," he said. "That's one name you ain't got and never will.'

"It's not a name yet," Bentz said. "It's just a handle."

"It will be," Dillinger said. "Just keep reading the papers, pal."

On the way back to the apartment on Halsted, Homer seemed depressed while Dillinger appeared in a strange state of exhilaration. Dillinger drove the Ford, taking Lake Shore Drive to Randolph, then headed south on Wabash to West Madison.

He laughed when they passed the corner of Dearborn. "This is really something," he said. "Don't this beat anything you ever saw. Bums, panhandlers, dope fiends, whores, pimps, bootleggers, queers. Christ, I never saw nothing like it. Makes you feel alive. Plenty of action all the time."

Homer nodded sadly. "Yeah, Johnnie."

Dillinger gave him a sharp look. "What's the matter with you?"

26

"Well," Homer said, moving as far away on the seat as possible. "I don't think you should have talked to Bentz that way. He's an okay guy. Could help us out a lot."

Dillinger made a wet sound with his lips and tongue. "Forget him. He's washed up. Nobody takes a cut from me without facing the action."

"We don't have no guns even."

"We'll get some. I've got it all worked out."

"Where?"

Dillinger laughed. "Some hick-town police station. Where else?"

Homers eyes lighted up. "Hey, Johnnie, that's great!"

"That's just the beginning. We're gonna hit a half dozen banks real fast. Pick up some dough and then spring the boys out of stir. After that we'll have our own organization."

"When're we taking off?"

"Tomorrow."

"Can I take Marie?"

"Can she drive?"

"Yeah, she's a swell driver."

"Let's take her. Might come in handy."

"Goddamn, Johnnie, this is great. I've been wondering when we'd swing into action. Man, I'm ready for it. My dough is running short."

Dillinger brought the car to a stop at the curb before the dingy apartment house. He turned to Homer and smiled, letting his hand drop on the thin shoulder. "How about sleeping on the sofa tonight, pal?"

Homer stiffened, his moist eyes worried. "What do you mean, Johnnie?"

"I mean sleep on the sofa. You're a little guy."

"Marie's gonna squawk."

"Why?"

"Well, she don't like the sofa."

Dillinger laughed good-naturedly. "Homer, wake up. She's gonna be in bed."

Homer's fat lips sucked air for a while, then he nodded.

The two men stepped out of the car and quickly went up the stairs to the third floor apartment. Marie opened the door, smiling coyly.

"Get me a drink," Dillinger said, dropping into the one easy chair ahead of Homer.

"Sure, sport. Gin or whiskey?"

"Whiskey straight with water chaser."

The coy smile was still on her face as she listened to the order.

"What's so funny?" he said.

"Why don't you go in the bedroom and find out," she said.

Dillinger jumped up, excited. "Evelyn?" he said, glancing at the closed bedroom door.

Marie nodded. "She's been waiting two hours. You better step on it."

"Hey, that's swell," Homer said, hurrying to Marie's side. "You can have the bedroom tonight, Johnnie. Marie and me will take the sofa."

Dillinger didn't wait to listen. In three giant strides he was at the door, flipping it open. "You Evelyn?" he said to the girl lying on the bed. "I'm John Dillinger."

"Come in, Johnnie," she said. "And close the door."

He closed the door and leaned against it, his yellow eyes carefully appraising her. She had on white lounging pajamas with a deep plunging neckline and a red ribbon in her peroxide-blond hair.

"Like what you see?" she asked, rolling over slightly, just enough for the neckline to fall open, revealing large cone-shaped breasts.

"I like it fine," Dillinger said, moving toward the bed. She patted a place next to her hips on the bed and he sat down.

"Go on and look at 'em," she said, pulling the material away from the breasts.

"Hell!" he said, his yellow eyes transfixed. "They're beautiful. Just like one of them Greek statues." Timidly, he reached out and curled both hands over the breasts. It was like touching cool marble, except that it was soft and pliable in his hands.

She watched him, her gray eyes amused. "Its been a long time, eh, Johnnie?"

28

"Too long," he said, caressing the brown nipples.
"You're cute, honey. Kiss me."

He kissed her, his hands now more demanding on her cool flesh. Her arms came up and gently pulled him down on top of her. "Keep doing that, baby," she said. "I like it."

Dillinger woke up twice during the. night, each time to stare arrogantly at the bar-like window frame before drawing up against Evelyn. And each time her eyes opened and her mouth found his hotly and wantonly in the darkness. They lay in each other's arms, silently touching each other, awakening the desire necessary to satiate their need.

They left the next morning, the four of them in Homer's Ford, with Dillinger driving and Evelyn cuddled up next to him, purring softly each time he touched her. Homer, sitting in the back, giggled happily, his moist eyes possessive again when he looked at Marie.

The year was 1933 and the month was June. The outlaw gangs of the Wild West had long since become legend. Jesse James, Billy the Kid, and the Dalton gang were all strange and exciting characters who had galloped across the prairies, leaving death and destruction in their wake.

The first two decades of the twentieth century had refined crime. It had placed it in the big city where ambitious politicians and tenderloin-eating cops could best protect it from society. Then, suddenly, the outlaw gangs were back, galloping across the prairies in long black Packards and sporty Ford V-8's, the six-shooter replaced by the Thompson submachine gun.

By the time John Dillinger decided to join the pack, bank robberies were occurring at the rate of two a day. Gun battles were an almost daily news item. Over two thousand hardened felons were on the prowl-across the length and breadth of the land, sacking a bank here, killing a cop there, kidnaping a rich man whenever one could be found in a country hovering perilously on the brink of economic disaster.

A dozen big names crowded the headlines: Francis Keating, Thomas Holden, Frank Nash, Alvin Karpis, Verne

Miller, "Pretty Boy" Floyd, Machine-gun Kelly, Ma Barker, Harvey Bailey, Earl Christman, Ray Terrill, and "Baby Face" Nelson.

Within fourteen months the name of John Dillinger would eclipse them all. His name would be blazoned across the newspapers of the nation. Children would imitate him, adults would shake their heads in bewildered wonder, and newspapers would reap the only true harvest of his exploits.

And then, as suddenly as it had started, it would end. John Dillinger would be dead, his straw hat and gun under glass at the FBI Bureau in Washington, his bullet-torn, blood-stained shirt placed on paid exhibition by a bereaved and confused father.

His remains would be interred under an impressive headstone in the Crown Hill Cemetery in Indianapolis, one of the largest cemeteries in the county. President Benjamin Harrison, Booth Tarkington, James Whitcomb Riley and three vice presidents of the United States would lie in state in the same hallowed ground.

For years Dillinger would remain the number one attraction, his grave trampled by thousands of the morbidly curious, his headstone slowly chipped away by the souvenir hunter.

And with his death a new legend would be born. A legend written with the speed of a ball-point pen on a full cartridge of blood.

They cruised across the northern sector of Indiana for four days, inspecting a dozen towns before settling on Auburn. Dillinger was in high spirits. Evelyn had been a rare find, far beyond his expectations. She was his kind of woman. She was beautiful, wanton and totally without scruples. The last four days had given him an opportunity to know her, to find out how the wheels turned in her beautiful head.

Though she had been earning well over a hundred a week at Ana Sage's brothel on Dearborn, she had walked out without a second thought. She was impulsive, gay and engagingly reckless. Nothing seemed to bother her. Her favorite saying clearly expressed her attitude toward life.

Once when the car had skidded dangerously around a curve, she had burst into peals of laughter. When Dillinger had questioned her about it, pointing out the danger, she had raised one thin, painted eyebrow and shrugged her fur-clad shoulders. "So what," she had said. "Here today, gone tomorrow. That's what my old pappy always said. And he was right." They had all laughed, secure in the thought that Evelyn had expressed a most profound truth.

The Auburn police station was perfect. It was small, dilapidated and badly understaffed. They sat in the car, directly across the street, planning the raid. It was a few minutes after midnight and the street was dark and empty.

"Stay in the car until I give you the high sign," Dillinger said, loosening his tie as he stepped out of the car. Bending down, he rubbed his hands in the loose dirt and carefully massaged his face. "How do I look?" he asked.

"Like Al Jolson," Evelyn said.

"Yeah," he said, going down on one knee, "Mammy!"

"Silly."

"Let me come, too," Homer pleaded. "I want to have some fun, too."

"Shut up," Dillinger said. "You come when I call you."

He winked at Evelyn and hurried across the street, quickly disappearing inside the building.

"He's okay," Evelyn said. "Got lots of moxie. I like that in a man."

"He's scared of nothing," Homer said. "You should have seen him in stir. Boy, he ran things around there. Johnnie's a real tough egg. He don't stand for no horsing around. You do what he says or you get your head busted wide open for you."

There was a bright glint in Evelyn's eyes as she straightened her fox stole. "I knew it," she said. "I knew it the minute I saw him. It's his eyes and his mouth and the way he uses both of them when he looks at you. I like that in a man."

A few minutes later, the door of the police station flew open and Homer saw Dillinger standing in the light, waving at him. They made three trips to the station, each time coming out with their arms loaded down, their pockets

31

bulging. The haul netted three submachine guns, two shot-guns, a high powered rifle, five revolvers, two automatics, a half dozen shoulder holsters, a couple of cartridge belts, boxes of ammo for all the weapons, and one bulletproof steel vest.

"We're in business," Dillinger said, as they sped out of town.

"Boy, oh boy," Homer cried, cradling one of the Tommy guns. "Rat-ta-tat-ta-tat—"

"Look out with that thing," Marie warned. "It might be loaded."

"Look at it, baby. Feel it. Boy, it's mine. Johnnie, let's stop somewhere and try 'em out, okay?"

Dillinger laughed. "Well, let's get out of town first. Those coppers ain't gonna be in dreamland forever."

"How'd you do it, Johnnie?" Evelyn asked.

He roared with laughter. "I did it with my trusty little Boy Scout knife. There were two screws in there. I asked for a place to wash and this dumb screw led the way down a long, dark hallway. I grabbed him from behind, you know, my arm around his neck and shoved the knife in his back. He just folded up. I took his rod and conked the other screw on the head with it."

"Did you kill him?"

"Who?"

"The one with the knife?"

"Naw. Didn't go in more than a couple inches down low. He got scared and wet his pants. Big tough cop."

They all laughed and Evelyn started singing the latest song hit, *Happy Days Are Here Again*. They sang it over and over again until they reached Bluffton some fifty miles south of Auburn. Dillinger drove along the main street, slowing down when they passed the First National Bank.

"This is it," he said. "We hit it tomorrow."

From the back seat, Homer giggled nervously.

The Bluffton First National Bank was a red brick struc-ture with ivy growing along its walls and a small patch of grass separating it from the paved sidewalk. Its doors

32

opened at nine in the morning and closed at three in the afternoon.

"How much dough you suppose they've got in that joint?" Homer asked, fingering the submachine gun on his lap as they lingered nearby in the car.

"I don't know," Dillinger said, his eyes fastened on the bank clock. "Whatever it is, it's more than we've got."

"Yeah, I'm just about broke. Boy, we sure been spending it lately."

"That's the idea, pal. Live it up while you can." He stopped, nudging Homer with his elbow. "Okay, remember now. I go in first. Give me thirty seconds and come in. And don't shoot that thing unless I tell you."

"Sure, Johnnie."

It was exactly five minutes to three when Dillinger calmly strolled into the small marble floored bank and approached the cashier. Except for an older man who was filling out a deposit slip at one of the tables, the bank seemed empty of customers.

The cashier looked up and smiled pleasantly. "Good afternoon, sir. May I help you?"

"Yeah," Dillinger said, his face pressed against the small bars of the screen. "This is a stick-up. Don't yell and don't press that buzzer if you want to stay alive."

The cashier, a thick-set man with a red face and blond receding hair, stared at him incredulously. "I beg your pardon," he said.

"Get up the dough," Dillinger said, "or I'll blow a hole right through your fat head."

At that exact moment, Dillinger caught sight of the uniformed bank guard coming out of the mahogany paneled holes occupied by the officers of the bank. A second later, Homer burst through the door, the chopper held waist high. The bank guard started to duck back inside the cubbyhole when Dillinger's voice stopped him.

"Don't move, sucker. Freeze."

For a fraction of a second, the bank guard seemed undecided, then, shrugging almost imperceptibly, he brought his hands up above his head.

33

"Watch him, Homer. All right. The rest of you monkeys stay put." He had the .45 automatic in his hand now and he was holding it steady, the barrel pointed directly at the cashier who appeared to be in a state of shock.

"You got sixty seconds to fill this bag," Dillinger said, handing him a brown paper sack. "Move or I'll blast you."

Suddenly, the cashier went into action, stuffing bills into the sack until his cash drawer was empty. He looked up, his eyes pleading for assurance that he had been a good boy.

Dillinger shook his head. "The other cages, pal. And be quick about it."

The cashier ran to the two tellers' cages with Dillinger following him on the other side of the counter. Dillinger was aware of the heavy silence, of the white staring faces, of the feeling that for the moment time hung suspended.

When the cashier finally handed him the paper sack, he took it in his left hand and moved back. "You were smart," he called. "All of you. Now just stay smart for another five minutes and nothing bad will happen to you." He turned and started for the door, passing by Homer without looking at him. Outside, he started the car, honked the horn and opened the door on Homer's side.

Then the shots came—a wild burst of machine-gun fire echoing down the sleepy street. Homer came out running and giggling, the chopper still jerking in his hand, the large plate glass window of the bank collapsing, the sound of glass as loud as the gunfire.

"Stop it," Dillinger hollered, the car already moving before Homer had even reached it.

"Johnnie," he cried, flinging himself into the front seat, the chopper clattering to the floor as he grasped for support. They raced down the street, careening around corners, finally disappearing in a cloud of dust.

The girls were waiting for them some eight miles out of town on a narrow dirt road. They were sitting on a small patch of grass, eating a picnic lunch.

Dillinger hadn't spoken a word to Homer during the entire ride. Homer, aware that something was wrong, had also kept his silence. The bag of bank notes lay on the seat between them, untouched.

"Oh, Johnnie," Evelyn trilled, running to the car.

Dillinger ignored her, reaching down for the chopper. "Get out," he said, pressing the barrel into Homer's side. Homer's face was wet with perspiration, his moist eyes flooded.

"Johnnie, what's the matter? What's wrong?"

"Get the vest out of the trunk," he said. "Put it on."

The girls stood quietly by as Homer donned the bullet-proof vest.

"Now, you gun-happy moron, I'm gonna show you what it feels like to get shot at."

"Johnnie, not the chopper, please."

"The chopper," Dillinger said. "Back up, you son-of-a-bitch."

It was the first time Dillinger had ever handled a submachine gun. Hamilton and Pierpont had talked so much about it in stir that it didn't even occur to him that it was his first time.

"Johnnie, for God's sake, what are you gonna do?"

There was a satanic grin on Dillinger's face as his yellow eyes narrowed and the black chopper swung up to his shoulder. "I'm gonna test that vest," he said. "It's supposed to be bulletproof." He sighted the Tommy gun like he had his deer rifle as a kid. "Don't move," he said. "Or you're gonna be without a head."

He touched the trigger lightly and a half dozen slugs smashed into the center of the vest, catapulting Homer backward, his arms flailing the air for balance. Encouraged by his first success, Dillinger stroked it for another short burst. Homer screamed and fell flat on his back, his legs kicking frantically.

Dillinger spun around and emptied the drum into the trunk of a pine tree, laughing, the bullets thudding into the bark, gouging out a pocket large enough for his fist.

The girls were kneeling beside Homer, their pale faces worried as they stared down at him. Homer was babbling incoherently and swiping at his wet nose and tear-stained

35

cheeks with balled fists, like a little boy who has been unjustly punished.

Dillinger stopped in front of the sprawled figure and pressed the muzzle of the chopper into Homer's unprotected stomach. The satanic grin was still on his face. "You're no good to me," he said. "I think I'll finish you off right now and leave your carcass for the vultures."

Homer sobbed uncontrollably.

"Aw, leave him alone," Marie said. "What'd he ever do to you?"

Dillinger gave her a cold stare. "Button it up," he said, "and keep it buttoned. This is business. The next time I tell him something and he don't listen, I'll kill him. You hear me, stupid?"

"Yeah, Johnnie, I hear you."

"Okay, so get up, and let's take a look at that vest."

"I'm all broken up inside," Homer whined. "It's like being kicked by a mule or something."

"You're alive, ain't you? That's what counts."

Dillinger examined the vest, pleased with what he saw. "Ain't damaged at all," he said. "That's okay."

"It weighs a ton," Homer said, sitting up. "Help me off with it, Marie. I think I made a knot in back here."

When they counted the loot—Dillinger was disappointed. It amounted to less than six thousand. The girls were happy.

"Do I get any of it?" Evelyn asked.

"Sure, baby. Here's a couple C-notes."

"Is that all?" she whined.

"Take it easy, baby. There's plenty more where that came from. This state is full of nice little banks. And when we're done here, there's always Ohio and Michigan and Illinois and Wisconsin. Don't worry. This is just the beginning."

CHAPTER FOUR

During the summer months—June, July and August of 1933—Dillinger and Van Meter cracked eleven banks, for a grand total of over a hundred thousand dollars. Two policemen, three bank guards, one vice-president, two tellers and one bystander were shot or otherwise wounded. No one was killed.

In early September, when the leaves were turning from red to gold, and the crisp autumn air was filled with the sweet pungent smell of burning leaves, they returned to Michigan City in two cars (Dillinger driving a dark blue Packard and Homer the black Ford), loaded down with sixteen pieces of luggage, five machine guns, thirteen assorted revolvers and automatics, six steel vests, four shotguns, three rifles and a case of mixed ammo. They looked tan, well fed and lively. The summer had been a smashing success. They had spent weeks at a lake in northern Wisconsin and had even visited Jack Hamilton's sister in Sault Ste. Marie, a small town on Michigan's upper peninsula. Hamilton had been more than a cell mate at Indiana State Prison. He had been his closest friend, the only man Dillinger had ever admired and respected.

While the two men waited in one car, the girls drove to a small motel on the lake front and rented a cottage. By this time John Dillinger was a wanted man, his name already familiar to headline writers in the midwest.

On one swing across the state in mid-July, Dillinger stopped at his father's farm for a few hours on a Sunday afternoon. The old man hadn't much to say. He thought Johnnie was making a terrible mistake and darkly prophesied imminent doom.

Dillinger proudly demonstrated the Tommy gun. By this time he could handle it with one hand and still hit

37

his target. His father scratched his head under the stocking cap and wiped his nose with his index finger, his old head shaking as if he had palsy. In one burst, Dillinger killed eight chickens and the nanny goat. Appalled by the wanton destruction, the old man ambled back to the house, with Evelyn running beside him, trying to console him.

"That nanny goat was my friend," the old man said. "The only friend I had left."

Dillinger heard the remark as he entered the room. "Here," he said, dropping two fifty-dollar bills on the kitchen table. "Buy yourself another one."

The old man began to rock in his chair, his fragile old jaw clasped tightly shut.

"What are you mad about? That damned old nanny goat wasn't worth the lead that killed it. It was just skin and bones."

The old man raised his eyes. "So am I," he said. "Why don't you shoot me?"

"Oh, for Christ's sake, Pa. Don't carry on about some stupid old goat like it was the end of the world or something. Here's a hundred dollars. Buy yourself a dozen of 'em if you're so crazy about 'em. Need any more dough? Just say so."

"You're the one that's crazy," he said. "You're crazy in the head, son. Bad crazy. Kill crazy."

"Ah, forget it," Dillinger said. "We've got to push on. I'll write to you first chance I get. Now, take care of yourself, you hear? I'll see ya."

They had left then but the old man had not come out to the porch to wave. Dillinger had written a few days later, enclosing another fifty-dollar bill. He had not received an answer.

The first two days in Michigan City were spent hiding in the motel, plotting the prison escape of his pals. The girls carted hot food from a restaurant down the street, but otherwise sat around quietly, their enthusiasm subdued by the tense-faced, hard-pacing Dillinger.

Once when Marie had turned on the radio, he had whirled on her, his hand raised threateningly. "Turn it off," he had snarled. "I've gotta think, damnit."

Homer, who had been completely cowed by the steel vest episode, did not venture opinions unless they were requested of him. And even then he hesitated.

"There's got to be a way of slipping guns into that joint without getting into the act ourselves," Dillinger said.

Homer nodded, biting his lower lip, his moist eyes blinking.

"Let's send them a big birthday cake with a chopper inside," Marie said, laughing nervously.

"Funny," he said, clamping his jaw, his eyes narrowed in concentration. "The idea is to get the guns on the spindle truck that goes right to the shirt factory where the boys work. There are two deliveries made from Chicago each week. Jack and Harry worked out a plan that's pretty good. Get the guns in one of the crates and mark it by coloring the heads of the nails with a red crayon. That way they'll know which crate they're in."

"That sounds like a good idea to me," Homer said.

"Yeah, sure. But how?"

"Well," Homer said, hesitating.

"Well, what?"

"How about hijacking the truck? You know, slug the driver and guard, put on their clothes and drive right into the prison—"

Dillinger held his head in dismay. "Oh, Jesus, will you shut up. You think those gate guards are blind or something?"

"No, but—"

Dillinger raised his hand for silence. "We've got to get to those crates before the truck reaches the prison. And we've got to do it without the driver and guard knowing about it."

"We need Charlie Chan," Marie said.

Dillinger spun around, his face contorted with anger. "Evelyn, take this nut out of here before I brain her."

"Let's go to a movie," Marie said.

"Okay, Johnnie?" Evelyn asked.

"Yeah, sure. Anything. Just get her out of here."

The girls left and Dillinger opened a bottle of beer. "Homer, this thing's got me licked. I've thought about it

39

all summer and I can't find no way into that goddamn joint. Christ, it's harder breaking in than it is breaking out."

"Well—" Homer said, again hesitating.

Dillinger flopped into an easy chair. "What's with you?" he said. "Lately, you can't say nothing without sucking air for an hour. Spill it."

"Well, I don't want to make you mad—"

"Who's mad? What's the matter, you cracking up or something?"

"No, Johnnie."

"Okay, then. Stop futzing around. Speak up like a man."

"Well, Johnnie, I was just thinking. All those boys need are guns. With guns in their hands they can blow their way out of that can like nobody's business."

"So?"

"Nothing. I was just trying to get it straight in my head. We don't have to worry about getaway cars or nothing like that."

"That's right. Get the guns to 'em and forget it. They'll take care of the rest of it."

"Maybe we could hold up the truck and just put the guns in there."

Dillinger jumped up, snapping his fingers. "That's it, Homer. But we don't hold up the truck. Christ, it's so simple it's funny."

"What is it, Johnnie?"

"We start trailing that truck on the next trip which is day after tomorrow. Then I'll show you what."

The thread company van pulled up at a diner just outside Porter, Indiana. The driver and guard climbed out of the cab and hurried inside the low-roofed building.

A moment later, a blue Packard pulled up behind the van and stopped in a position that completely hid it from the diner window. Homer and Dillinger jumped out of the car and the two women casually strolled toward the diner. Homer climbed up on the van's tail gate, pushed the hanging tarpaulin aside, and quickly hid behind it. Dillinger passed him a small cardboard box—filled with six revolvers and a short crowbar.

40

"Which crate?" Homer asked from behind the canvas.

"Any crate," Dillinger said. "Just don't forget to mark it with the crayon like I told you."

Homer nodded, already busy at work. Dillinger got back into the Packard and drove away, parking directly in front of the diner door. On the floorboard by his feet was a submachine gun. He lit a cigarette and leaned back in the seat, tipping his hat forward, his eyes narrowed and watchful.

It was a simple plan. If the driver and guard were still in there when Homer returned, then they would both go in and get something to eat as if nothing had happened. If they started coming out before Homer was finished, the girls would warn him ahead of time and he would rush into the diner with the chopper and fake a robbery, holding everybody at bay until Homer returned. Either way, the driver and guard would have no reason to suspect anything wrong with their shipment.

Inside the diner, the driver was eating a cold beef sandwich and the guard a hamburger. Evelyn and Marie sat next to them at the counter, sipping coffee. Marie looked at the driver a moment, then broke into a big smile.

"Hey," Marie said, tapping the driver's hand. "Don't I know you. Ain't you from Chicago?"

"Yeah," the driver said, winking at his buddy. "I'm from Chicago, sweetheart."

"That's what I thought."

The guard leaned forward for a better look. "I'm from Chicago, too," he said. "What are you girls doing around here?"

"Just traveling. My name is Alice and this is my friend, Norma."

"Glad to meet you girls," the guard said, taking the play away from the driver. "I'm Pete and this is Oscar. He's a truck driver and I'm a guard."

"What do you guard?"

He laughed. "Nothing much, I guess. We go to the penitentiary in Michigan City and I make sure nobody bums a ride in or out."

They all laughed and in the excitement Marie furtively

41

brushed against the driver. "Hey," she said. "How about sitting in a booth and getting acquainted?"

The guard pulled out his pocket watch and carefully examined the black hands. "Don't have too much time," he said. "We're on a tight schedule."

The driver shook his head. "Don't worry about it, Pete. We'll make it up on the road."

"No," Pete said. "Can't take the chance."

"Party pooper," Evelyn said, pouting prettily. "And I thought you were cute."

"So are you, baby. Give me your address and I'll drop in on you in Chicago."

"Nuts," she said. "I don't like you."

"Business is business," he said. "You dames just don't understand things like that. Always la-di-da and stuff like that. Us men have to earn a living.'

"Oscar ain't worried about the silly old schedule," Marie said.

"Oscar's a stud," Pete said. "He can't think of nothing else when dames are around."

Marie blinked her eyes rapidly. "Oh, Oscar, I had no idea."

Oscar blushed from his shirt collar to his hat brim. "Pete, cut it out, will ya?"

"It's true, ain't it? This guy's a terror with women. You can't tire him out."

"You're terrible," Evelyn said. "We're nice girls and don't like to hear such talk. It's dirty."

"No insult intended," the guard said. "I just thought you girls would like to know a thing like that. It can be important sometimes."

"That's all right," Marie said. "Don't listen to her. I'm interested. Tell me more."

The guard poked Oscar and laughed. "Maybe, sometime, he can show you gals. Know what I mean?"

Behind them, the door swung open and Dillinger and Homer strolled in and casually selected a booth.

"Okay. Some other time," Marie said. "We don't want you boys to louse up your schedule."

"Thanks for nothing," Pete said, then turned to Oscar. "Come on. We're wasting time. Let's get out of here."

That evening they packed up and drove out of Michigan City, stopping overnight in Toledo. They were on their way to Dayton, Ohio, to visit a friend of Evelyn's.

In New Carlisle, some twenty miles north of Dayton, with the girls waiting in the car in front of the bank, Homer and Dillinger swung into the Commercial Trust and relieved it of $3,500.

Front page headlines greeted their arrival in Dayton. A blurred picture of Dillinger, taken in the penitentiary some five years earlier, accompanied the account of his exploits.

Then the impossible happened. Acting on a tip from a neighbor, four burly detectives quietly sneaked in with a passkey and caught John Dillinger asleep in the bedroom of their new apartment. He lay on his back, fully dressed, a holster gun under each armpit and a full cartridge belt around his waist. When he woke up, two cops had his arms pinned back, grinning down at him, while the other two were very thoroughly going through the contents of the dresser drawers.

"That's a nice toy," one of the cops said, picking up the submachine gun hidden under the bed. He whirled and aimed the gun at Dillinger's chest, his eyes narrowing as if he meant business. "What if I had an accident?" he said. "My finger slipped or something. Bang, bang. Good-bye, Mr. Bigshot."

"You son-of-a-bitch," Dillinger yelled, struggling futilely to break away from all the weight and muscle holding him down. "I'll get you for this. I'll get you if it's the last thing I do."

"All you gonna get is twenty years, buster," the cop said. "We'll see to that."

Fighting and shouting, Dillinger was led out of the apartment and thrown into a police car. That day he got his first national headlines.

The next morning he was promptly arraigned and trans-

43

ferred to the county pail at Lima. It was there, a few days later, that he read of the escape of his pals from the Indiana State Prison. The story was the first bright spot since his capture. Sprawled out on his bunk, grinning, he carefully read and re-read the news account:

TEN SHOOT WAY OUT OF PRISON

MICHIGAN CITY, Ind., Sept. 26—Ten desperadoes shot down a clerk, slugged a guard, kidnapped a sheriff and a motorist, menaced two prison officials with death and escaped today from the Indiana State Penitentiary.

Successful in what appeared to have been a long-plotted break for liberty, the convicts sped away toward Chicago, 55 miles distant, in two automobiles commandeered from the men they abducted.

Two of the fugitives were serving sentences for murder and four for robbery; all six had been given life terms. The others were serving maximum sentences of twenty-five years for robbery or automobile banditry. They were regarded as the most dangerous men in the prison.

The escape started in the prison shirt factory. Assistant Warden Albert Evans was summoned to the shop on the pretext that he was needed there because of breakdown in machinery.

GREETED BY GUNS

He was greeted on arrival by six men with pistols and four with clubs. The convicts disarmed Evans and forced him and D. H. Stevens, plant superintendent, to accompany them.

Taking with them a ten-foot steel shaft for use as a battering ram if needed, the ten prisoners forced Evans and Stevens to accompany them into a ventilating tunnel running under the prison building.

After a "council of war," each of the desperadoes picked up a bundle of shirts and they marched up into a cell block. Each guard then encountered was told by the escaping men, "We're taking these shirts out." Menaced by pistols concealed beneath the bundles of shirts, Evans and Stevens could not give a warning.

Half a dozen iron doors were opened in that manner and the procession filed through. Finally they reached the guard room, one wall of which formed part of the main gate of the prison.

At this point, two guards, Guy Burklow and Fred Wellnitz, questioned the group. Wellnitz was slugged into unconsciousness ·

44

by pistol butts. The desperadoes then ransacked the prison arsenal, taking possession of machine guns, rifles, shotguns and bulletproof vests. Burklow was then forced to open the outer gate.

CLERK WOUNDED

Looking for money, the convicts entered the prison clerk's office outside the wall. One of the half dozen clerks in the office, Finley P. Carson, became confused and failed to observe a chorus of orders shouted at him.

Bullets struck him almost simultaneously in the leg and in the shoulder. The desperadoes finished ransacking the office and fled when they heard an alarm sounded inside the prison.

As they fled, they encountered Sheriff Charles Neel of Corydon, Ind., who had just brought several prisoners to the penitentiary. They overpowered him, took his weapons, and forced him to carry four of them away in his automobile.

A short distance down the highway, the others forced the driver of an automobile carrying two women to head his car into a ditch. They rode away with the driver.

Warden Lewis H. Kujkel and Chief Clerk H. C. Crosby gave the names of the escaped prisoners as: James Jenkins, Edward Shouse, Russell Clark, James Fox, Walter Dietrich, Joseph Burns, Harry Pierpont, Charles Makley, John Hamilton and James Clark.

An immediate investigation to determine the means by which the pistols were smuggled into the prison was announced by Warden Kujkel. "As yet we don't know how these men got those guns," he said. "But we aim to find out very quickly."

CHAPTER FIVE

Louis Phillip Piquett was a mouthpiece extraordinary.

Once the city prosecutor of Chicago in the heyday of Al Capone, Piquett, by 1933, had branched out into a field of criminal law that required forensic abilities he did not possess.

Using the contacts made while in office, Piquett was on

good terms with fixers, politicians, hideout owners, gangsters, abortionists, bootleggers, dope pushers, madams, pimps and a colorful array of contact men reaching all strata of the underworld.

Short and pudgy, with a shock of white hair that stood nearly two inches above his broad forehead, Piquett made a formidable appearance in court. Short of arms and heavy-paunched, his cheeks jowled and his chin wattled by fat, he could be belligerent or maudlin at will.

His courtroom tactics consisted of constant wranglings over minor points of law, badgering of opposing attorneys, wild, irrelevant interrogations, intermittent speeches denouncing law enforcement officials, and exhausting orations to the jury accompanied by heart-rending sobs and real liquid tears.

Piquett and Dillinger distrusted each other on sight. Hired by Homer and Marie to defend Dillinger in Ohio, the Chicago lawyer immediately drove down to the county jail in Lima to interview his new client. Evelyn Frechette, posing as Piquett's secretary, came along with him and was admitted to Dillinger's cell.

Smiling sympathetically, Piquett looked the other way while they comforted each other in an unusually long and noisy embrace. Afterwards the two men talked, slowly at first, feeling each other out for weak spots like two cautious club fighters.

There was a half-mocking smile on Dillinger's face as he listened to Piquett's ponderous explanation of the legal technicalities involved in the case.

"Identification at the scene of the crime is direct evidence," he said. "Most difficult to contradict in court. It wouldn't be a bad idea for you fellows to wear masks in the future. Make it a lot easier in court later on. How many people do you suppose saw you with that gun in your hand?"

Dillinger sneered. "I wasn't counting. Maybe ten, maybe fifteen."

Piquett shook his head, ramming his stubby fingers through his white hair. "I can't understand why you fellows don't cover up. What's the point? It's irresponsible."

"The point is I don't figure on getting caught."

"But everybody gets caught, sooner or later. It would be a lot later if you fellows used your heads and covered up."

"You've made your point," Dillinger said. "What do we do now?"

"We fight, of course. I haven't had time to check the hand my opponent is holding as yet but I will. Then I'll let you know what's what."

"Stall for time," Dillinger said.

"What in the world for?"

"I like it here," he said. "It's nice."

"You're a peculiar fellow, Johnnie."

"Mr. Dillinger," he said. "Only my friends call me Johnnie."

"Why, aren't I your friend?"

Dillinger shook his head. "Not yet, pal. Not yet."

"I'm sorry to hear that, Mr. Dillinger. Nevertheless, I'll see what I can do for you. Meanwhile, I'll try to delay the trial as long as I possibly can." He turned to Evelyn. "Now, I think we better go, my dear."

"Take it easy," objected Dillinger. "Smoke a butt and relax. I've got something urgent to discuss with Evelyn."

Piquett forced a polite cough. "By the way," he said, "my fee is five thousand dollars, with an immediate retainer of two thousand."

"See Homer. And look, pal, how about turning your head the other way. What I have to say is kinda private, know what I mean?"

"Yes, indeed," he said, stroking his white hair, his black marble eyes glinting knowingly.

In the next two weeks Dillinger read the newspapers avidly. From the dozens of accounts of his exploits, a new image of John Dillinger was beginning to emerge. It was a strange image, not all like himself, and he wondered about it, trying to understand the intangible meaning he somehow sensed between the lines of each new story.

Most of the writers appeared sympathetic, almost as if they were trying to justify his deeds. One long, sad story told of his youth, depicting his poverty at great length, his

47

father's hardships, stating how he had lost all of his savings in the crash when the local bank had failed and how that same bank was now trying to foreclose the mortgage on his small farm.

This, the story pointed out, was one of John Dillinger's reasons for becoming an outlaw. He was trying to redress a wrong. Seeking revenge against a common enemy—the rich bank owner. Dillinger was another Robin Hood. A Pancho Villa. A poor man fighting the powerful rich in the only way open to him. The law had been unjust to him by sentencing him to an unusually long prison term for a minor offense when he had been just a mere boy.

Anecdotes were printed about his mistreatment in prison, dwelling on the sadistic guards who had beaten him with clubs and whips. Prison officials had twisted him with their brutality, transformed him from a simple farm boy into a hardened criminal. Now society had to bear the brunt of its mistake.

Dillinger liked what he read. He liked it and encouraged it by granting interviews freely. He talked of his poor father who was so old and so alone, and who strove so bitterly hard to keep body and soul together. He had been a slave to the land and to the bank all of his life. And now, in his old age, he had nothing to show for his efforts. It was unfair, unjust and un-American. The newsmen went for it the way a cat goes for catnip.

On the evening of October 12, Sheriff Jesse Sarber was seated behind his desk in the jail office. His wife Lucy and Thomas L. Sharpe worked at nearby desks.

When the front door opened the sheriff casually glanced up at the three men entering the jail. He leaned back in his chair and pushed his hat to the back of his head. "Any thing I can do for you fellas?" he inquired.

Harry Pierpont nodded importantly. "Yeah, Sheriff. We're Michigan police officers and we want to see John Dillinger."

Sarber's eyes narrowed quizzically. "Let me see your credentials."

"Sure thing, Sheriff," Pierpont said, reaching inside his

48

jacket and coming out with a .45 automatic. "Here are my credentials."

"What are you—"

"Let him have it," Charles Makley said.

Still smiling, Pierpont squeezed the trigger, sending a slug crashing into the sheriff's chest. Sarber sat there a moment, his eyes wide with surprise, then slowly slumped in the chair and slid to the floor.

Lucy Sarber jumped up, screaming.

"Shut up," Russell Clark shouted, grabbing her by the arm and roughly pushing her back in the chair. Makley quickly moved up to cover Deputy Sharpe.

"All right, you two," Pierpont ordered. "Take us to the cell block. Hurry."

Sheriff Sarber groaned softly and his arms reached out on the floor before him. "Bastard," Pierpont growled, viciously striking the sheriff on the head with the gun butt. "Now, let's go."

Deputy Starke led the way to the steel door leading to the cell tiers. He stood before the door, his hand trembling so he couldn't insert the key in the lock.

"Quit your stalling," Pierpont warned.

"Sorry," Starke mumbled. A moment later the key slid into the lock and the door swung open.

Pushing their two hostages before them, the three outlaws hurried into the bull pen. Dillinger stood in a corner of the room with a dozen men around him.

"Come on, Johnnie," Pierpont said.

Dillinger ran up to them, laughing. They all shook hands, clapping each other on the back.

"What are you doin' in the pokey, Johnnie?" Pierpont asked, winking at Makley and Clark.

"Vacation," Dillinger said. "Needed a little rest."

"Let's get out of here," Makley said. "Before we all get a rest."

Locking in Lucy Sarber and Deputy Sharpe with the rest of the prisoners, they made their way back to the sheriff's office and broke into the gun rack, taking three submachine guns and other firearms and ammunition.

49

"What happened to him?" Dillinger asked, pointing to the body of the dead sheriff.

Pierpont gave a loud shrill laugh. "We showed him these credentials," he said, waving the .45 automatic. "These he liked."

"That's right," Clark said. "No argument."

"Very co-operative," Pierpont added.

"I'm surprised you didn't bust out of this tin can by yourself, Johnnie," Makley said.

Dillinger's eyes hardened but he smiled. "Easier this way," he said. "After all, one good turn deserves another. By the way, where's Jack?"

"Getting things set up in Chicago. Sends you his greetings."

Dillinger nodded, turned and walked out of the jail, the three men falling in line behind him. Without saying a word, Dillinger had automatically assumed command of the outfit.

This prison break, carried out in a matter of minutes, had no rival in history. And what followed in the next nine months was even more unprecedented.

Louis Piquett received Dillinger back to Chicago with opened arms. Through one of his underworld contacts, he provided a hideout for the gang on South Halsted Street. It was a small vacant red-brick rooming house with fancy iron grillwork in the front. Dillinger appropriated a three-room apartment on the first floor and left the assigning of the other rooms to the discretion of Jack Hamilton, whom he had selected as his lieutenant.

Hamilton, known as Three-Finger Jack, had been the first important con to recognize Dillinger's leadership ability in stir. They had bunked in the same cell block and had become close friends in the last three years of Dillinger's confinement. Dillinger had had great admiration for Hamilton's sharp, incisive mind. Jack had a way of looking at a problem with a fresh and unusual approach that never failed to excite the younger man. Hamilton was forty-one years old, of medium height, stocky, with dark hair and black piercing eyes.

Charles Makley, at fifty-two, was the oldest member of

the gang. Double-chinned and barrel-chested, Makley looked every inch the part he had elected to play in life. Russell Clark was ageless, of medium height and weight and colorless. He was the original copy of the invisible man. Harry Pierpont was over six feet tall, a thin wiry man with sandy hair and light gray, mocking eyes. He was the most educated (college degree in engineering) and the most dangerous, having been classified as a pathological killer by the prison psychiatrist.

Once comfortably settled in the rooming house with all their baggage, armament and mistresses, the boys decided to throw a party to celebrate the two prison escapes.

Invited to the party as guests of honor were Louis Piquett and Ana Sage—Piquett for his legal and illegal assistance, and Sage for her contribution of Marie Conforti and Evelyn Frechette to the Dillinger gang. By this time two other molls had joined the entourage: Mary Kinder with Pierpont and Opal Long with Clark.

Piquett brought a friend to the party. "This is Dr. Joseph P. Moran," he said, introducing Dillinger to the most notorious doctor in the Chicago underworld.

"Everybody calls me Doc," Moran said, weaving slightly, trying to concentrate his glazed eyes on the man before him.

Dillinger looked sharply at Piquett. "Doc likes a little drink now and then," Piquett said, smiling, his arm draped affectionately across the doctor's shoulder. "Best damn sawbones in Chicago. Good men to know, Mr. Dillinger."

Dillinger shook Moran's hand. "Call me Johnnie," he said. "You, too, Louie."

"Listen, Johnnie," Doc said, holding on to Dillinger's hand. "What you need is a good surgeon like me to work on you."

"What for? There's nothing wrong with me."

"Afraid of the cops, aren't you? Well, you can go anywhere without worrying after I've done a lifting job on that face of yours. I'll alter that nose, change the shape of it entirely. Then I'll lift those cheeks. Change the expression of your eyes. Raise your eyebrows. Take the sag out of your mouth. They'll never know you." He stopped, minutely examining Dillinger's fingertips. "Well, I can fix these, too. Nothing to it."

Dillinger pulled his hand away and stepped back, his eyes flashing. "What is he? A nut or something?"

"I beg your pardon," Moran said, insulted. "I'll have you know, sir, that I was an honor student at Tufts Medical School and I was decorated in France for my work with badly disfigured soldiers. I made them look human again. I created them all over again. Like an artist. A sculptor. No. Like God."

"It's true," Piquett said. "Doc here is a fine plastic surgeon."

"I don't need it," Dillinger said. "And let's get one thing straight, Doc. I ain't afraid of the cops as you said before. I ain't afraid of nobody. And don't you ever forget it."

"I need a little drink," Doc said, staggering away to find a bottle.

Piquett laughed. "As I said before, Doc's a good man to know. A man never knows when he's gonna be sick."

"Or get lead poisoning," Dillinger added.

"That's right. The kind of business you and your friends are engaged in at the moment is what a prudent man might call a trifle hazardous."

"Talk English," Dillinger said. "Save those big words for Capone."

"*Touché,*" Piquett said, looking about him, his marble eyes amused at the drunken spectacle. "The boys seem to be having a good time. How do you like the place?"

"Okay, but a grand a week is too high."

"Johnnie, hideouts cost money. This is the best buy in town. Believe me, I know."

"Hell, this whole building ain't worth a grand."

"Don't kid yourself. This building is worth its weight in gold. Know why?"

Dillinger shook his head.

"It's in the twenty-first ward."

"So?"

"So, Johnnie, it's in my back pocket. I run this ward. All the way from the alderman on top to the beat cop on the bottom. You can sit on the front stoop with a machine gun in your lap and a big sign on your chest with your name on it and the cop on the beat will look in the other direction. It's the way things are run around here. That's what ninety per cent of that grand is buying. Protection."

"It's still a lot of money."

"Later, when you become a killer and the feds are on your tail, a thousand will be chicken feed."

"Honey, come join the party," Evelyn said, taking his arm. "We're all gonna sing, '*Happy Days Are Here Again.*' You, too, Louie."

"Just a minute," Dillinger said, glaring at Piquett. "You got a real big mouth," he said.

"I was merely being realistic," Piquett said. "Look, Johnnie, you're not the first bank robber I've had for a client, you know. You keep robbing banks with machine guns and sooner or later somebody's gonna get killed. Like Sheriff Sarber got killed in Lima. It just happens."

"So it happens. So what. Anybody who gets killed is asking for it. We don't kill for nothing. The Sarber thing was self-defense."

Piquett smiled. "Okay, Johnnie. Now I think we should go sing with this charming young lady who looks so lovely hanging onto your arm."

"What a line," Evelyn said, rolling her eyes.

They sang, drank and danced. Sometime around two o'clock, Homer and Marie went out looking for chop suey and hamburgers.

Opal Long did a strip on top of the dining table; Evelyn, cuddled on Dillinger's lap, made the muscles of her buttocks quiver as she French-kissed him. Mary Kinder bared her breasts and Doc Moran came up and examined them carefully, his pale fingers more sensuous than professional in their probing. Pierpont looked on, laughing maniacally.

Louis Piquett cornered Ana Sage and, while he kissed her, she ran her fingers through his long white hair, her enormous oval eyes closed, the mascaraed lids like twin shrouds. Russell Clark stood by the table, staring up at Opal, egging her on to a more obscene display of her opulent charms.

53

Makley lay stretched out on the floor, his head propped up against the wall, a half-empty bottle of gin resting on his chest.

In a small room on the second floor, Jack Hamilton had expertly dismantled a .45 caliber Thompson sub-machine gun. His black eyes gleamed fondly as he carefully cleaned and oiled each small part laid out on the bed before him. A radio blared loudly at his side, drowning out the shrieks and laughter beneath him.

He could think best when his hands were occupied. His meeting with Johnnie had been a lot different than he had expected. The kid had changed. But how he had changed was something Jack couldn't quite figure out. He just couldn't put his finger on it. He had been friendly, happy to see him; and he had not questioned his not coming to Lima with the other boys. Still, there was a definite change. A change in the expression around the eyes, the set of his mouth, and the tone of his voice. It was all very peculiar and puzzling. It was as if an invisible wall had been erected between them.

They talked and laughed as always. And yet every time Jack said something important it seemed like the words just bounced against that wall and dropped dead at his feet. Maybe the kid wasn't listening, he thought. At least, not the way he'd listened in that old cell when they used to talk half the night away. Then, he had been interested, asking wild questions, making Jack repeat the details of some past heist over and over again.

He had been an eager and bright student. It had been obvious that his experience was limited. But experience wasn't everything. The kid had something better than experience. He had the will to lead men. Place him in a group of strangers for just ten minutes and he naturally took over without anybody even suspecting it. You would tell him one thing today and two days later he would repeat it to you as if he had just invented it. And he gave orders in a manner that left no doubt in the receiver's mind.

Now he was becoming a big man in the public eye. Only his name had made the headlines in the story of his escape from the Lima jail. Though Pierpont and Makley had been identified by the deputies, their names had barely received a mention in the story. The kid had been out of prison not even five months and already he was a big man. A bigger man than any of them would ever be.

This thought didn't disturb Hamilton. Being boss did not interest him. All he cared about was doing the jobs and doing them correctly. The bank heists Dillinger had been pulling were reckless to the point of being ridiculous. Nobody with any brains swung into a bank without knowing the whole score. To do otherwise was more than stupid —it was plain suicide.

Now that they were a gang, things would have to be organized. Every job would be planned and carried out with professional skill. No more cowboy stuff. That was for jerks. Johnnie would have to listen, or else.

Johnnie did listen. He listened for a good fifteen minutes before blowing his top. All six men were in Hamilton's room, some were seated on the floor, while others leaned against the wall. Dillinger stood in the center of the room, his shirt-sleeves rulled up, his collar unbuttoned, the two holstered guns black and menacing under his armpits.

"That kind of junk sounds ókay in stir," he said, pointing a long, still finger at Hamilton. "But it don't go here. Every bank in the country is jittery. You move into some hick town and start casing a job and you're dead inside of twenty-four hours. There's only one way to heist a bank and that's to go in and clean it out without no goddamn fuss. Homer and me been doing just that with no trouble."

"Johnnie," Hamilton said. "You've been pulling two-bit capers. I'm talking about big-time stuff. A hundred grand a touch. Nothing smaller."

"Yeah. The papers don't think it's two-bit stuff."

"Ah, crap on the papers. What do they know?"

"They know me," he said.

"So. That don't make you right."

"Look, you guys want in or not?" Dillinger queried.

"Sure, Johnnie, we want in. But now we got a six-way split. Nobody's gonna risk his neck for a ten-grand swag cut six ways."

"That makes sense," Dillinger said. "I don't want a ten-grand swag either. I've got big jobs lined up in a half dozen towns in Indiana."

"Great," Hamilton said. "But that's another thing, Johnnie. From now on we've got to spread them out. Hit one in Indiana, the next in Ohio, then to Wisconsin, to Illinois. Keep 'em guessing."

Except for Homer, Dillinger wasn't sure how the men were reacting to the argument. None of them had spoken up. They were awaiting the outcome silently, leaving the decision to the best man.

"All right," he said. "The first job is the Greencastle, Indiana, National Savings and Trust. From there we go right to Racine, Wisconsin, and double back here to Chicago for a job."

"Okay, that sounds fine to me," Hamilton said. "When do we hit it?"

"October twenty-six. That gives us a week."

"I'll leave tonight with Homer," Hamilton said.

Dillinger stared at him for a long time, his piercing eyes unblinking. "Jack," he said softly. "You're pushing me. I don't like it."

Hamilton shook his head. "I'm not pushing, Johnnie. It's your party all the way. I just want to buy a little life insurance for all of us. Try it my way once. If you don't like it, we'll do it your way next time. Fair enough?"

Dillinger could feel the tension dissolving in the room. Jack's concession had restored his authority. Now he could go along with the plan without losing face. He looked sternly at Hamilton, then at each of the men. "It better work," he said. "That's all I've got to say."

CHAPTER SIX

Greencastle was a small town with a big bank, some fifty miles southwest of Indianapolis. With Homer behind the wheel of the Packard, Hamilton explored the country roads leading in and out of town. Then, with a yellow foolscap pad on his lap, he accurately laid out the getaway chart.

Setting the odometer at zero, they drove away from the bank, clocking the distance between turns, marking down easily identified landmarks, and the maximum speed possible on the turns as well as on straight stretches and curves.

During the actual getaway, a member of the gang would sit in the front seat by the driver and read off the instructions, keeping one eye on the odometer and the other on the chart, calling out the speeds and turns. The chart completed by Hamilton covered a distance of sixty-eight miles, and provided the shortest and fastest route out of Indiana and into Illinois.

Working out the chart took two full days of hard work. The next step of the job took Hamilton to the public library. Here, seated comfortably at a table, he thumbed through the files of the local newspapers until he found the bank's published statement of assets and liabilities.

Noting down the cash on hand, the cash due from other banks, the amount owed the Federal Reserve, the bond inventory; making allowances for withdrawals, for changes since the date of publication, he was able to determine the approximate net balance available in the vault.

Satisfied that there was close to a hundred and forty thousand dollars awaiting them in the vault, Hamilton paid his first visit to the bank.

Dressed in a conservative business suit and derby hat, with a brief case under his arm and pinch-nose spectacles softening his piercing black eyes, Hamilton easily assumed the bearing of an important businessman, worthy of the attention of at least a vice-president.

The subject he wanted to discuss concerned the possibility of starting a new business venture in Greencastle, the nature of which he was not free to disclose at the moment. It was still under wraps at the main office. His interest was in the financial stability of the largest banking institution in Greencastle. Under these circumstances, the vice-president was only too happy to give him the grand tour, proudly pointing out the fortress-like impregnability of the bank—which, of course, included a close inspection of the alarm system, the thickness of the steel vault (and information about the hours it was open during the day), the armed guards and their stations.

Visibly impressed, Hamilton thanked his gracious guide profusely and departed a much wiser man.

Dillinger listened, nodded, grunted, but refused to be impressed. Makley, Pierpont and Clark were much impressed and quick to show it. They hovered around Hamilton, laughing and slapping him on the back, all talking at once as they studied the physical layout of the bank which had been meticulously drawn to scale on a piece of yellow foolscap.

"The best time is twelve-forty," Hamilton said. "At that time, all the bank officials, except for one vice-president, are out to lunch. The cashier is out and two of the four tellers. The beat cop drops into the drugstore for a sandwich, and more than half the police force is scattered to the four winds, feeding their faces. As far as the alarms are concerned, we might have some trouble there. All the cages have floor buttons, including the cashiers' and the three vice-presidents'."

"How about the guards?" Dillinger asked, hoping he had found a flaw in the plan.

"I was coming to that," Hamilton said. "There are two guards but only one is on duty at that time. He stands close to the main door, greeting the customers and looking everybody over pretty damn careful like. He's gonna have to be dealt with right from the start."

58

"Anything more to add?"

"No, Johnnie. That about covers it."

"Okay, here's how we do it," Dillinger said. "You guys get around me here and listen good while I lay this caper out." He paused, his yellow eyes flashing. "We're gonna hit this crackerjack box so fast they won't know what happened till next Christmas."

At exactly twelve-forty the next day, Jack Hamilton entered the Greencastle National Savings and Trust, attired in his now familiar business suit and derby hat. The bank guard smiled pleasantly and Hamilton nodded, touching the brim of his hat in greeting. He walked across the empty lobby, his footsteps echoing on the marble floor, and stopped before the mahogany railing which led into the clerical section. One of the clerks hurried over, a pinched anxious smile pulling at the corners of his thin mouth.

"Good morning, sir. Can I be of service to you?"

"Good morning. I'm Mr. Stevens. I believe I have an appointment with Mr. Goodfellow."

"Oh, yes, sir. Mr. Goodfellow is expecting you. This way, please." He swung the small railing gate open and escorted Hamilton to the vice-president's office, tapping lightly on the door. The door was opened immediately by a beaming Mr. Goodfellow.

"Come right in, Mr. Stevens. Please have a seat." He closed the door and turned to face a .38 special aimed squarely at his chest. "Why, why, Mr. Stevens. What's the meaning of this?"

"Shut up," Hamilton snapped. "This is a holdup and you do what I tell you, or I'll kill you."

Mr. Goodfellow leaned weakly against the closed door. "Please, don't hurt me," he said.

"Nobody's gonna hurt you if you follow orders. Understand?"

"Yes, sir. I think so." His hands had begun to tremble and his knees sagged dangerously.

"Open the door and call the guard in here. And smile when you do it. Now go on. Open it."

Mr. Goodfellow swallowed with great difficulty. "Mr. Higgins is going to think this most peculiar."

"He better not. Now call him. You've got five seconds." Hamilton tripped back the hammer, the clicking noise sharp and deadly in the silent room.

Mr. Goodfellow spun around and swiftly opened the door. "Mr. Higgins," he called, his voice cracking with fear. "Will you come to my office immediately?"

As the guard disappeared into Mr. Goodfellow's office, Dillinger and Pierpont entered the bank, each going to a separate teller. The tellers were away from their windows, talking together through the wire mesh screen separating their cages. They were both standing at least three feet from the alarm button, totally unaware of the bandits' approach until Dillinger barked at them.

"Freeze," Dillinger said, pointing two .45 automatics at the tellers.

"Don't move a muscle," Pierpont ordered, also holding two automatics.

"Okay," Dillinger said. "I've got these crums. You round up the clerks."

The door to Mr. Goodfellow's office opened and Hamilton waved to Pierpont. "Bring 'em all in here," he said. "On the double."

Seven frightened clerks and two tellers were ushered roughly into the office and lined up against the mahogany paneled wall along with the guard and Mr. Goodfellow. Pierpont went back to the lobby to cover any customers who might come in.

Ten seconds later, Makley and Clark strolled into the bank, each carrying a large cloth sack.

"Let's clean it out," Dillinger said, leading the way behind the railing. "Clark, you take the cages. Charlie and me will take the vault."

Three customers came in during the robbery and were promptly marched into the vice-president's office. Otherwise, there were no interruptions.

Seven minutes from the time Hamilton had entered the bank, the job was finished and the men had disappeared without a single shot being fired or a blow struck. Inside the two cloth sacks was a grand total of one hundred and forty-four thousand dollars. Four thousand more than Hamilton had originally estimated. One hour and fifteen minutes later they crossed into Illinois.

They drove directly to Racine, Wisconsin, where the girls had already rented a furnished house in a middle-class neighborhood on the south side.

Though it had been a beautifully executed job, perfect in every detail, Dillinger was not pleased with the result. The take, bigger than all of his previous jobs had produced, did not help the situation. While the boys drank and joked on the ride north, Dillinger sat in the back seat, strangely quiet, his cruel eyes staring out of the car window, unaware of the early winter snow gently blanketing the countryside.

Hamilton sat next to him, his black eyes distant, as if in thought. Pierpont, Clark and Makley played with the money, tossing handfuls of it at each other like confetti. Now and then a bill floated down in front of Homer's moist eyes and he giggled hysterically.

"What's the matter, Johnnie?" Hamilton asked after a while. "Something bothering you?"

Dillinger shook his head and continued to stare out the window.

Hamilton shrugged and reached out for a bill, grasping it tightly in his fist. "Look at it, Johnnie," he said. "See, it's green."

"Don't bother me."

"It's good, you know. You can spend it anywhere."

"Ah, leave him alone," Pierpont said. "He don't feel good."

"What's the matter, Johnnie? Did it go too smooth for you?"

"Shut up," Makley said. "Now, goddamnit, leave Johnnie alone."

"No," Hamilton said. "There's something wrong here and I want to know what it is."

Dillinger turned slowly in the seat, his face as hard as stone. "Jack," he said coldly. "You better take a nap. You look tired."

61

"Johnnie, this was your job. All I did was case it. You planned it and the credit is all yours. Right, fellas?"

They all loudly voiced their agreement.

"The whole thing went off like clockwork. Hell, you should be happy."

"It had no class," Dillinger shouted. "No goddamn class at all."

Hamilton stared at him, turning puzzled eyes to the other men. "I don't get you, Johnnie. What d'you mean, no class? It had plenty of class. As much as any job Eddie Bentz ever pulled. This was a real pro job."

"I don't know what I mean," Dillinger said, turning back to the window. "Now leave me alone. I've gotta think about this."

They pulled two more jobs· in the next two weeks: Racine and New Castle, Ohio. They were all clean jobs, expertly engineered by Hamilton. On November twelfth they arrived back at the old rooming house on South Halsted Street in Chicago.

Meanwhile, the Dillinger image was growing all out of proportion in the Corn Belt press. His exploits and possible whereabouts were subjects of daily interest to millions of readers. Despite the publicity, Dillinger remained sullen. He read the papers, his lips moving as his eyes slowly scanned the words. Later, Evelyn carefully clipped the items and pasted them in the large scrapbook he had bought that summer in Indianapolis.

Stories of the adventures of other desperadoes did not interest him except when cops or bank officials were murdered. Of all these stories, the Kansas City Massacre had pleased and excited him the most. He had bought all the newspapers available and had sat ¯and listened to Evelyn's reading of the detailed accounts with flashing eyes and curled lips.

He had particularly enjoyed the part in Union Station where "Pretty Boy" Floyd had shouted, "Up! Up!" to the˓ cops before cutting loose with his machine gun. Backed by Verne Miller and Adam Richetti, Floyd had then shouted, "Let 'em have it." And with that command the three gunmen, cradling choppers, had opened fire on seven policemen, killing four of them instantly and wounding two others. One of the men killed and the two wounded were FBI agents. Another special agent had miraculously escaped injuries. The cause of the attack, Frank Nash, who had been in transit to Leavenworth prison, died with a bullet in his head from the gun of one of his eager liberators.

The Urschel kidnaping in Oklahoma City had no interest for Dillinger. He figured snatching a dumb racket when there were so many banks just waiting to be cracked.

The capture of Machine-gun Kelly in Memphis, Tennessee by FBI men had thoroughly disgusted him. Kelly had been captured without firing a single shot. The way it sounded in the paper, the tough guy who could knock walnuts off a fence with a machine gun at twenty-five paces, had dropped on his knees and begged: "Don't shoot, G-men!" In his anxiety, he coined a new word that swiftly caught the nation's fancy.

Others had made the headlines in that period. "Baby Face" Nelson, who had escaped from Joliet in the summer of 1932, had moved his field of operation from the Northwest to the Midwest, with three recent bank robberies chalked up to his credit.

The Barker-Karpis gang kidnaped Edward G. Bremer of St. Paul and collected a $200,000 ransom. The search for the kidnaper of the Lindbergh baby still made an occasional headline. Al Capone was transferred from Atlanta to the new Federal Prison erected on that bleak rock known as Alcatraz, in the San Francisco Bay. And in all those months not a single word was written about Eddie Bentz.

Life in the rooming house on South Halsted continued at a gay, mad clip. There were parties and poker games which lasted through the night. There was drinking, dancing, laughter and singing and a great deal of dallying and love-making.

The girls paraded around in every stage of dress and undress, observing very little decorum in their behavior or speech. Evelyn joined in all the fun, up to a point.

63

Dillinger was her exclusive property and she refused to share him with any of the other girls. Though she romped naked like the others at certain parties, no one dared make a pass. It was an unwritten law, understood by all.

Dillinger stared in awe whenever she went into one of her jealous screaming rages. Once, in a state of drunken stupor, she had allowed another woman to sleep with them. The next morning when she realized what had happened, she bombarded him with a string of invectives known only to a former Dearborn Street prostitute. Dillinger had laughed it off, calling her back to bed, where they spent most of the day in tender reconciliation.

There was only one flaw in the honeyed ointment—Jack Hamilton. He hovered over Dillinger, discouraging one wild escapade after another, preaching caution at every turn.

Movies, night clubs, dance halls, restaurants, department stores, bowling alleys, pool parlors, anything that was fun became automatically taboo. Sometimes Dillinger listened, and at other times he scoffed and jeered and went out anyway. What was the use of all that money if he couldn't go out and enjoy it once in a while? Every day the rooming house became more like a prison and the window frames more like iron bars.

The toothache started in the middle of the night. He woke up moaning, his hand pressed tightly against his jawbone, and sat up in the bed. A few minutes later he was rocking wildly, nearly out of his head with the pain. At his side, Evelyn stirred and slowly opened her eyes.

"What's the matter, honey?" she asked, snapping on the lights, and leaning forward to look at him.

"It's a tooth," he whined. "It's killing me."

"Let me see."

"Don't touch me," he cried. "Oh, Christ, I'm dying. My head feels like it's gonna blow up."

"I'd better call Doc."

He closed his eyes tightly, wrinkling his nose, his lips curling up over his teeth. "Do something," he screamed. "Just don't sit there like a goddamn dummy. I'm dying, I tell you."

64

She jumped up and ran from the room, her naked white buttocks shaking. He could hear her high frantic voice, and he gritted his teeth and pounded the side of his mouth, the sharp pain lancing through him like hot needles. Then she was back in the room, cradling his head against her bare breasts, rocking, her voice soft and soothing.

It took Doc Moran an hour to get there. By the time he arrived Dillinger had consumed nearly a quart of whiskey and was beyond pain. He sat limply in an easy chair, his arms dangling over the sides, his head sagging against his chest.

"Now, what have we here?" Moran inquired, gingerly lifting Dillinger's head and prying his mouth open. With a small flashlight he examined the tooth, shaking his head and muttering to himself.

Evelyn, her nakedness covered by a thin silk wrap, stood anxiously at his side, trying to decipher the doctor's mumbling.

"What's wrong?" she finally asked when he had finished his examination.

"Very bad," Moran said, his hands flat on his hips as he bounced up and down on tiptoes. "Impacted. Going to need some oral surgery."

"Wisdom tooth?"

"What else? Must have been coming on a long time. Didn't he mention it before?"

"No. This is the first time."

"Okay. I'll make arrangements with a dentist and call you back later."

"Can't you take care of it?"

He shook his head, still bouncing on his toes. "Not my line."

"Can you give him something for the pain?"

Moran laughed. "He's got the best medicine in the world right now. He'll be okay till morning."

Homer drove and Hamilton sat in the back with Dillinger. The effect of the liquor was wearing off and the pain was gradually returning. He sat with his hand gripping his chin, his eyes staring balefully out the car window.

"I don't like it," Hamilton said. "Doc wasn't sure of this guy. Might be he got wise and called the cops."

"Jesus Christ," Dillinger said through clenched teeth. "Don't you ever let up?"

"Somebody's gotta worry around here. There are rewards for our scalps, Johnnie. Big fat rewards. There's not a guy in this country who don't know your mug. This goddamn headline crap has made you as famous as Roosevelt."

Suddenly, Homer's head perked around, his moist eyes wide with panic. "Cops," he shouted. "They're crawling all over the place."

Dillinger and Hamilton dove for the floor and the machine guns lying there at their feet.

"Let's get out of here," Dillinger shouted. "Step on it."

The car shot forward, careening dangerously as Homer jockeyed it through the busy downtown traffic. A moment later, bullets thudded into the car, shattering glass and puncturing holes in the thin metal body.

Dillinger and Hamilton opened fire simultaneously from each side of the car, shooting indiscriminately in all directions.

The car shrieked around a corner on two wheels, nearly going out of control. "Watch it," Hamilton warned. "Look where you're going, you stupid ass."

Dillinger broke the rear window, propping the muzzle of the chopper against the steel frame. "Come on, you bastards," he cried. "Come and get it."

A moment later a siren wailed behind them and a patrol car skidded around the corner not more than a hundred yards behind them, gaining steadily.

"Slow down!" Dillinger shouted. "I want a crack at 'em!"

He knelt on the seat, cheek pressed against the wooden stock, left eye closed and the other narrowed to a slit as he sighted down the barrel. Slowly, he squeezed the trigger, the gun throbbing in his hands, the bullets splattering into the front of the patrol car.

"Higher!" Hamilton shouted. "Get the windshield."

Dillinger's finger stayed frozen on the trigger. A moment later the windshield of the patrol car exploded. Dillin-

66

ger kept shooting even after the patrol car had veered sharply to the right and jumped over the curb, crashing into the brick wall of a building.

"Stop it," Hamilton warned, poking him in the ribs. "You'll burn out the barrel."

"Didja see that," Dillinger cried, laughing. "Wham! Man, that'll teach those bastards to come gunning after John Dillinger."

"Slow down," Hamilton said to Homer. "We've lost 'em. No need to attract attention. Turn left at the next corner and let's get back to West Madison where the cops are a little more friendly."

Dillinger sat with the hot chopper in his lap, grinning happily. "Damn," he said. "I don't even feel the tooth any more."

They abandoned the car near Lake Shore Drive that evening. There were twenty-eight bullet holes in the body, not counting the broken windows. His objections overruled, Doc Moran lanced the abscessed gum and extracted the impacted wisdom tooth. Dillinger stayed in bed, under sedation, for two days, his jaw swollen and his eyes bloodshot from the pain.

On Christmas Eve he drove down to Mooresville with Evelyn, Homer, Marie and Hamilton. Marie, Evelyn and Dillinger's sister cooked the Christmas dinner with food brought from Chicago. The old man sat quietly by, his faded blue eyes constantly moving across the strange faces.

They had brought champagne, whiskey, cigars and fancy little appetizers. There were toys for his sister's kids and a wool shirt and leather boots for his father. The girls were very domestic, humming Christmas carols as they bustled about the large kitchen, squeezing the kids every chance they got.

At dinner the old man said grace and every head bowed respectfully. Dillinger carved the large turkey, a cigar clenched in his teeth, the two guns hanging under his armpits. There were a half dozen machine guns scattered about the house, creating an impossible temptation for his sister's boys.

After dinner the men moved to the parlor to smoke cigars and nap while the girls cleaned up the kitchen. The radio was tuned to Christmas music. At five o'clock there was a newscast, announcing the capture of Edward Shouse in Peoria, Illinois. Shouse was one of the ten men who had escaped during the break at the Indiana State Prison.

"Shouse stated after his arrest," the announcer said in a deep, dramatic voice, "that he had not seen John Dillinger in over a month . . ."

Dillinger jumped up and turned up the sound. "That fink," he said. "He ain't never seen me."

". . . If you policemen are married men," the announcer said, quoting directly from Shouse's statement, "with families, I warn you to be careful about trying to take the other boys. They'll shoot it out to the last bullet and they have plenty of guns and bullets."

"You're not just joking there, fink," Dillinger said, glaring at the radio. "Where does that bum get off with that crap?"

"Wants to be a big man," Hamilton said.

"Yeah, that's right. Riding on my shirttail, the crum."

After that, Dillinger's spirits flagged. The girls fixed coffee and pumpkin pie with whipped cream but the fun had gone out of it. They bedded down early and drove back to Chicago just as dawn was breaking across the snow-covered horizon.

CHAPTER SEVEN

The next job was something completely different from anything they had done in the past. The idea had occurred to Dillinger one night while he was out on the town with Evelyn. They had stopped at the Beverly Gardens, a night spot on Southwestern Avenue. Dillinger had liked the place, impressed by all the well-dressed patrons and the prices on the menu.

"Look at 'em," he had said. "All rich and fat. No problems. I'll bet they don't even know who I am."

That night in bed he thought about it and first thing the next morning he called a meeting of the gang in Hamilton's room.

"We're gonna hit the Beverly Gardens," he said. "And we're gonna hit it New Year's Eve, the biggest night of the year."

They all seemed stunned. He waited for a reaction, his eyes traveling from face to face.

Hamilton was the first to speak up. "New Year's Eve is tonight," he said. "That don't leave us much time for planning."

"We've got all day," Dillinger said. "Besides, I thought about it all night. We hit it like any bank. Choppers and steel vests. There's one main entrance and one exit backstage. Half the guys go in the front and the other half through the back. We get everybody lined up and skin 'em. Then we hit the safe in the office and the cash register in the front. What could be more simple?"

"Sounds good to me," Homer said.

"Me, too," Makley agreed.

"Count me in," Pierpont said.

"Same here," Clark said.

"How about you, Jack? Want to take a rain check?"

Hamilton shook his head. "We'll need more guys," he said. "There's gonna be a big crowd tonight. We don't want any wise guy pulling a rod and plugging one of us in the back when we're not looking. Be some cops around for sure."

"Got anybody in mind?"

"Yeah, Walt Dietrich and Joe Burns. They're in town. Want me to call 'em?"

"Later, first let's get this organized."

"There's gonna be a lot of heat after this caper."

"Fellas, don't worry about it. We're gonna take ourselves a little vacation after tonight. I understand Miami is pretty nice this time of year. Besides, I'm sick of the snow

69

and cold. We leave right after the job. The girls will have everything packed and ready when we swing by here for them.

"What time do we hit it?"

Dillinger grinned. "At midnight. Right on the dot. When everybody is sloppy drunk."

"Yeah," Pierpont said. "*Auld Lang Syne* and all that crap."

The M.C. tolled off the countdown to midnight, accompanied by cheers, yells, horn blasts and the general caterwauling of hundreds of little mallets beating against hundreds of little tin pans.

"Happy New Year everybody," he screamed above the noise. "It's midnight, nineteen hundred and thirty-four." He raised his arms for the band and began singing in high tenor voice: "Should old acquaintances be forgot—"

"This is a stick-up everybody! Get your hands up!"

Several things happened in that split second. The band died in the middle of a note; the M.C. stopped with his mouth still opened, the sound just a gurgle in his throat; a man with his hand inside a girl's dress whirled about so quickly he snapped the shoulder strap, unveiling one gorgeous but very startled breast; a nervous waiter dropped the entire contents of a silver tray on top of a vile-tempered dowager in an original French creation.

Suddenly, eight men holding machine guns had completely surrounded the room. The patrons stared at them wide-eyed and bewildered, slowly huddling together in the center of the room for protection.

One of the armed men, attired in a brand new tuxedo, stepped forward, grinning. "Happy New Year, suckers," he said. "I'm John Dillinger. We're here for your money and nothing else. You do like I tell you and nobody's gonna get hurt. If you don't, I'll kill you.

"Now line up, all of you, right in the middle of the room. There's a man with a gunny sack there. That's Homer Van Meter and he's got a mean temper. You drop all your jewels and money in that sack. You can keep your wallets. Just

70

make sure you get all the dough out. After that you walk to the bandstand and two men will check to make sure you're not a wise guy. If they find even a nickel on you, you're gonna get slugged. Now, start moving and be quick about it."

Dillinger lit a cigarette and stuck it in his mouth, his eyes moving warily about the room, ready for action at a second's notice. It was a long slow process, but orderly. Nothing happened until fifteen minutes later.

Then all hell broke loose. Policemen burst through the door, armed with riot guns, shouting orders.

"Let 'em have it," Dillinger shouted, cutting loose with the Tommy gun, the cigarette still stuck in his mouth, the grin still on his mocking face.

The first cop in the room went sprawling, his face bathed in blood. The noise of the guns and the screams of the frightened people was deafening. Dillinger ran across the room, grabbing Homer by the arm, pulling him toward the rear exit according to plan, which called for a mass retreat in one direction.

The idea was that nobody, but nobody, could stand up to the concentrated fire of eight machine guns. Walt Dietrich came running, then stumbled, dropping to his knees, the chopper clattering to the floor as he grasped his stomach, his eyes surprised as he looked up at Dillinger.

"I'm hit, Johnnie," he gasped. "Below the vest."

Dillinger grabbed him by the hair and pulled with all his strength. "Get up and walk out of here, you bastard. Go on, move."

Dietrich staggered to his feet and reeled backstage, his arms still wrapped around his stomach, his body doubled over. Joe Burns caught a slug in the left ear, ripping muscle and cartilage, the blood spurting out in a crimson stream.

In the alley they found more cops. Pierpont came dashing out, his machine gun blazing, his maniacal laugh sending chills down the cops' spines as they frantically ducked behind ash cans or tried to scratch holes in the solid brick walls on each side of them.

A moment later they fled, their riot guns useless against

the firepower of a half dozen choppers. Pierpont's laugh followed them every step of the way, the slugs from his gun ricochetting off the brick walls with a deadly pinging sound.

The last cop out got it right in the back. It was as if a giant hand had smashed him in the small of the back, breaking his spine with one blow. He stopped in midair, like somebody doing a reverse jackknife, the back of his head slapping against the heels of his shoes.

"Jesus, did ya see that?" Pierpont yelled. "Son-of-a-bitch!" By now everyone was in the car except Pierpont. "Get in here," Dillinger shouted. Pierpont leapt as the car shot by, barely reaching the running board. Makley and Clark pulled him inside.

"Man, that was something," Pierpont said. "I mean it was really something. Cut him right in half. Just like a buzzsaw. Zip. Did ya see it, you guys?"

"I saw it," Hamilton said. "It was stupid. That poor guy was on his way home. He wasn't gonna cause nobody no trouble."

"He was a cop, wasn't he?" Pierpont screamed. "A dirty, lousy screw, wasn't he?" Pierpont's eyes had swelled and his lips were pulled tight across his teeth.

"Yeah, he was a cop."

"Well, the hell with you, Jack. I don't like cops. I kill 'em. Now, don't give me no goddamn crap. Right, Johnnie?"

Dillinger reached out and patted his shoulder. "Right, Harry. I saw the bastard go. Broke him right in two. Good shot."

Pierpont's face relaxed, his eyes glinting brightly in the darkness. "Son-of-a-bitch," he murmured to himself. "That was *really* something."

There were no soup kitchens nor bread lines nor shanty towns in Miami Beach in 1934. But there were other things —things like snow-white buildings, huge picture windows, chrome-plated elevators, jewel-bedecked heiresses, swivel-hipped gigolos, bald-headed tycoons, and swarthy-faced hoodlums. And then there were octagonal cabanas, candy-striped umbrellas, salt-scented surf, warm golden sand, and

72

inextinguishable sunshine as gentle as a ripe Florida orange.

The Dillinger gang moved in en masse, taking possession of an entire floor of a southwest wing in one of the most exclusive hotels along the beach front.

In the daytime, they frolicked in the water and in the evening they made the rounds of the night clubs all the way to Key West. Liquor was legal again and the night clubs presented specialty acts designed to titillate the most prurient palate.

Gambling was wide open. All the clubs had back rooms, featuring crap tables and roulette wheels, plus chuck-a-luck and slot machines. Dillinger went for the crap tables. Once he started gambling, he couldn't stop. He stood at one table over nineteen hours and dropped fifty-eight thousand dollars. Hamilton, standing next to him, dropped nearly forty thousand. Homer quit after thirty.

Evelyn threw a screaming, raging fit and cried the entire night. In the morning, exhausted and nearly broke, Dillinger got together with Homer and Hamilton.

"We need some dough," he said.

They nodded sadly. "Let's hold up that joint," Homer said. "Like we did in Chicago."

Hamilton shook his head. "No holdups around here," he said. "There's no way out of this state. With a half dozen roadblocks they could box us in forever. Know how far we are from the state line?"

"No."

"Five hundred miles."

"Let's go back to Indiana," Dillinger said. "I've got a bank all picked out. And this time, Jack, we do it my way."

"What's the bank?"

"The First National in East Chicago."

East Chicago, situated on Lake Michigan near the Illinois state line, was the seventh largest city in Indiana. Though it had a population of only 40,000, it was a fairly cosmopolitan town with very few hayseeds in its slicked-down hair. Its twenty-mile proximity to Chicago gave it the sheen of a prosperous suburb.

73

With his overcoat draped over the machine gun under his arm, Dillinger stepped out of the car and quickly crossed the sidewalk with Hamilton directly behind him. Homer stayed in the car with a machine gun under a blanket on the front seat.

In the vestibule, Hamilton waited as directed while Dillinger strolled into the lobby. A moment later, the overcoat dropped to the floor and Dillinger swung the machine gun up to waist level and shouted: "This is a stick-up. Put up your hands, everybody."

A dozen employees and two guards were swiftly rounded up before the ugly snout of the chopper.

"Okay, Jack," Dillinger said, waving to him.

Hamilton moved swiftly. He ran into the lobby, leapt over the guard railing, and immediately started filling a leather grip. From the corner of his eye Dillinger caught the movement of Walter Spencer, a vice-president of the bank, as he reached under one of the desks and pressed a button. The chopper went off almost simultaneously with the alarm, the slugs whistling above Spencer's head.

Two uniformed cops ran up to the front door, peered through the glass, saw the machine gun aimed in their direction and ran back for cover. Hamilton stopped, a pinched look on his hard face, his cold black piercing eyes undecided.

"Go in and get it, Jack," Dillinger said calmly. "That jerk there gave the alarm and the cops are outside. But don't worry, get all the dough. We'll kill all these coppers and get away. Take your time."

With one hand Dillinger lit a cigarette, his face relaxed, his eyes moving from the glass door to the assembled employees.

"The vault is locked," Hamilton shouted from the back.

"You, there," Dillinger said, addressing Spencer. "Unlock it."

Spencer shook his head. "It's a time lock," he said. "Won't open until three o'clock."

Dillinger stared at him a moment, then signaled to Jack. "Take this jerk along," he said. "We'll teach him a lesson."

74

Hamilton shoved a .45 automatic in Spencer's back and pushed him out ahead of him.

"Get it all?" Dillinger asked.

"All that's out."

"Listen, sucker," Dillinger said, poking the muzzle of the chopper into Spencer's chest. "You go out ahead of us. Any trouble and you get it."

Spencer nodded, his white face beaded with perspiration. "Okay, let's go."

There were eight policemen in front of the bank when Dillinger and Hamilton hit the sidewalk. The car was gone. With Spencer in front of him, Dillinger swung the chopper to cover the police officers who were armed only with pistols.

"Don't you screws make a move," he said. "Or I'll kill this guy and blow the rest of you to hell."

"Please, fellows," Spencer said, his voice high and pleading. "Do as he says. Don't make him mad."

Policeman William P. O'Malley took one step forward. "Dillinger," he said, "we'll get you for this."

"Get back there with the rest of the screws," Dillinger said. "And shut up."

O'Malley stood his ground, the .38 special in his hand aimed at Spencer and Dillinger. "There's eight of us," he said. "And only two of you."

Dillinger laughed harshly. "Try it, screw," he said, swinging the chopper away from Spencer and aiming it directly at O'Malley. "Now get back like I told you, or you're gonna get it."

Slowly, O'Malley stepped back, his face beet-red as he glanced at his fellow officers.

A moment later they heard the roaring of the car and Homer brought it to a squealing halt at the curb. Smiling smugly, Dillinger turned his head and something hard smacked into his back.

O'Malley fired four rapid shots, the slugs bouncing off Dillinger's steel vest, before the other officers even knew what was happening.

"You son-of-a-bitch," Dillinger snapped, whirling about.

"You've asked for it and now you're gonna get it." The chopper barked angrily and O'Malley slumped to the pavement, dead before his head hit the concrete.

Swinging the smoking chopper to cover the rest of the policemen, Dillinger carefully backed into the car and waited for Hamilton to get in. Then with Spencer on the running board, the car pulled away from the curb and sped down the street with Spencer's coattail flying in the wind. Not a shot was fired at the fleeing bank robbers. Two blocks away Hamilton pushed Spencer off the running board while the car was doing forty miles an hour. He landed on the street, bounced a couple times and rolled wildly under a parked car.

Minutes later they crossed the Indiana state line into Illinois. They headed straight for Chicago without spotting one police car. ˋ

Dillinger and Hamilton counted the swag which amounted to $20,376.

"Not worth it," Hamilton said.

"We got away, didn't we?"

"Yeah, but they've got a murder rap on you now. It just means that much more heat. And there's enough goddamn heat as it is."

"Forget it. We'll go meet the gang in Tucson and really raise hell. Cheer up, pal."

Hamilton shook his head sadly. "We could have a good thing going for us," he said. "I don't know why you don't listen."

"I've got a good thing. You worry too much."

"Somebody's got to worry. Christ knows you don't."

"You're damn right I don't. I say live it up. Here today, gone tomorrow. That's what Evelyn always says. And that's the way I figure it."

"I want to be here tomorrow," Hamilton said.

"Then you're in the wrong business, pal."

"That's where you're wrong, Johnnie. I belong in this business. Not you. You don't belong in this business at all. You never did."

"Read the papers tonight," Dillinger said. "You'll see who belongs in this business."

76

"I'd rather read the funnies," Hamilton said. "It's more believable."

"What's the matter, Jack? You jealous?"

Hamilton shook his head. "Johnnie, I can't talk to you no more. There was a time when I could. But no more. You've got it all figured out and it's all ass-end-to."

Dillinger looked out the window. "Times have changed," he said. "I was green in those days."

"Sure, you was green. But you made sense. You don't no more."

Dillinger didn't answer.

"What d'ya think? You think you can't get killed like the next guy? You think that steel vest is all you need to stay alive?"

Dillinger laughed. "That was a funny feeling getting hit like that. Didja see the look on that copper's face when I didn't fall down dead?"

"Dietrich had a vest and got it right in the guts."

"He ain't dead."

"No, but he could be. The only point I'm trying to make, Johnnie, is to take it easy. Don't let the papers make a patsy out of you."

"What d'ya mean by that?"

"I mean, don't let those monkeys push you out on a limb. They'll saw it right out from under you."

"Nobody's pushing me anywhere. I know what I'm doing."

"I don't think so, Johnnie. I think you're all mixed up inside. You've been reading all them screwy stories about what a big man you are and you're trying to live up to it. You can't, Johnnie. Nobody can. It's easy for a guy to sit at a desk and write fancy words about you, making you some kind of a dare-devil nut. Doing it is something else."

"What d'ya mean? You saying those stories are phonies? Like hell, they are! I've done all them things they write about me. And more. They don't know the half of it." He stopped and grinned crookedly. "Hey, Jackie, they ought to see me in bed."

Hamilton slapped Dillinger's knee. "Well, I don't think I got anywhere, but at least we've had some kind of a talk. That's better than nothing."

77

"Jack, you're the one that's screwy. We talk all the time."

"Not like we used to. Not any more. Now we argue and bicker. But we don't talk."

"You're crazy."

"Yeah, I know."

"Oh, Jesus Christ. You're my best friend. You know that."

"Then why don't you listen to me?"

"I said friend. Not mouthpiece."

"Okay, Johnnie. It's your skin. Don't say I didn't warn you."

"Here, have a butt and shut up, will ya?"

They smoked in silence, each looking out of a window. They were driving through Chicago's Near North Side, crossing Bughouse (Washington) Square, when they heard the siren. Dillinger sat up straight, his head cocked slightly to the side. "Turn right," he said, tapping Homer. "Take Delaware and move it."

Homer didn't need any additional prompting. That wailing sound behind him was all he ever needed to make tracks. The patrol car went barreling down Clark, seemingly unaware of them.

"Turn north on LaSalle," Dillinger said.

Homer turned to nod just as a car pulled away from the curb. There was a loud metallic crushing sound and the squeal of brakes.

"What are you stopping for?" Hamilton shouted. "Get out of here."

Confused, Homer accelerated while his front wheel was still locked with the twisted bumper of the other car. The automobile spun around, skidded, bounced against parked cars on the other side of the street, and then shot out like a rocket. Two blocks away the front tire blew with the impact of a shotgun blast.

"In the garage," Hamilton ordered, pointing to a four-story garage to his right.

"Gonna ruin the tire," Homer said.

"Screw the tire," he snapped angrily, turning to Dillin-

78

ger. "Johnnie, this jerk gets stupider every day. We've got to do something about him."

Dillinger was staring out the back window. "There's a cop coming," he said.

"Probably don't know it's us," Hamilton said. "Saw the accident and is coming over to give us a ticket."

Dillinger gave a short laugh. "I'll give the bastard a ticket."

The car wobbled into the garage and the three men bounced out, machine guns and leather grip in hand, and ran to a large black limousine.

"Get in," Dillinger said, pushing Homer behind the wheel.

"Jesus," Homer said. "The keys are in it."

"Let's go," Dillinger said, already in the car. "Come on, Jack."

Hamilton came around from the other side of the car, running hard.

"Hold it," Policeman William Shanley called from the garage entrance.

Hamilton spun around and fired as he moved, the shots going wild.

Shanley quickly went down on one knee and calmly returned the fire. Hamilton gasped and slumped against the car, still firing as he sank slowly to the floor. Shanley's body jerked violently and the gun dropped from his hand. With superhuman effort, he stood up and took a half dozen steps backward before dropping to his knees. He died that way, kneeling on the pavement, his head between his knees.

"Jack," Dillinger cried, leaning over Hamilton. "You okay?"

He nodded. "Help me up," he whispered. "I can't feel my legs."

Homer jumped out of the car and helped push Hamilton into the back seat of the limousine. Three or four employees stood at the other end of the garage, watching fearfully, frozen into immobility.

They drove slowly out of the garage and down Michigan

79

Avenue with Hamilton on the floor of the limousine, the blood seeping from his side and running in a tiny stream on the plush gray carpeting. Dillinger sat above him, his hand pressed against Hamilton's side, just above the hipbone, trying to stop the bleeding by applying pressure to the wound. Behind them there was a scurry of activity in the garage, the shouts and yells of onlookers hurrying to the scene.

"Want me to step on it, Johnnie?" Homer asked.

"No."

"He's bleeding pretty bad."

"Drive and shut up."

"Okay, Johnnie."

Hamilton opened his eyes and the bright hard sheen was gone. He smiled faintly and closed them again.

"Does it hurt, Jackie?"

"Not bad. I feel drunk. My head is spinning like crazy."

"Take it easy. We'll get Doc to patch you up."

Hamilton scratched feebly at the steel vest. "Take it off, Johnnie," he whispered. "It's crushing me. Too heavy."

Dillinger rolled him on his stomach and quickly untied the vest. A moment later he removed it and dropped it on the seat.

"That feels great," Hamilton said. "I can breathe again."

"You'll be okay, Jackie. It's nothing serious."

Hamilton tried to smile but kept his eyes closed. "That damned slug feels as big as a rock inside me."

Dillinger cradled Hamilton's head in his arm, wiping the saliva that drooled from the corners of his mouth.

"Remember stir?" Hamilton asked. "I took care of you then. Lot of cons didn't like you but I stood up for you and they came around to my way of thinking." He stopped and took a deep breath. "We're pals, Johnnie?"

"Sure, we're pals. Now, take it easy, will ya?"

"Don't leave me," Hamilton said. "I don't wanta die alone."

Dillinger gave a harsh laugh. "Who's gonna die? It's nothing, I tell you. Doc will have it out in no time."

Hamilton nodded and opened his eyes. They were piercing-sharp for a moment, then slowly faded, a film settling over them like a dark cloud. "It's all a lot of crap, Johnnie. All crap."

"I'm telling you. It's nothing."

"No, Johnnie. Not that. I mean us. You know, life. It's all a big pile of crap." He closed his eyes and slowly sank into unconsciousness.

CHAPTER EIGHT

The fire broke out shortly after midnight. Evelyn woke up and sat bolt upright in the bed, her eyes wide as she sniffed the acrid, pungent smoke that was slowly seeping through the crack under the closed door.

"Johnnie," she cried, shaking him awake. "The damn joint's on fire."

"What?" He sat up, his nostrils dilating, his eyes wide as they searched the darkness.

He had been in Tucson three days. Hamilton was back in Chicago, bedded down in the rooming house, with Homer and Marie watching over him. Doc had removed the slug which had miraculously missed the left kidney and large intestine. The operation had been performed on the kitchen table while Doc had been half crocked. Dillinger had stood by, determined to kill him if the operation failed.

The death of the two policemen, Shanley and O'Malley, had generated a lot of heat. It had made bold headlines across the country. Driving alone from Chicago to Tucson, Dillinger had bought newspapers in every town he had gone through. The back of the car was stacked full with them by the time he arrived in Tucson. Even the wire services had carried the story. Newscasters on the radio had dramatized the incidents even beyond the pale of fiction.

81

Dillinger had taken his time driving down, stopping only at the best motels. Twice he had halted to ask directions from a policeman, a gun in his hand, ready to shoot if he were recognized. But the trip had been uneventful. Marie had bitched about going back to Chicago but Dillinger had forcibly put her on a plane.

There was no doubt about it. It was smoke. Dillinger stood up and walked naked across the room to the window, opening it. Evelyn, also naked, ran after him. "We've got to get out of here," she cried, grabbing him around the waist and pulling with all her strength. A' moment later they heard the clanging of bells and the shrill wailing of sirens.

"Jesus Christ," Dillinger shouted, trying to disengage himself from her fierce grip. "Let go, damnit!"

She was crying, a wild look on her face. "I'm afraid of fire," she sobbed. "Take me out of here, Johnnie. Please."

Angrily, he raised his hand, his eyes flashing. She stared up at him, pleadingly. His hand stopped in midair and his face softened.

"Don't be afraid," he said. "I won't hurt you."

She pressed herself against him, her mouth sinking into his neck.

"I love you," she murmured. "Oh, Johnnie, Johnnie. Love me."

His arm snaked around her shoulder and he pulled her against him, crushing her bare breasts against his chest.

Outside, fire trucks growled to a stop and the sound of excited voices drifted up to the opened window.

"We'd better get out of here," he said. "Come on. There's nothing to worry about. I'll take care of you."

Still holding on to her, he moved across the room to the closet. When he let her go, she was smiling up at him with tears in her eyes. "I'd do anything for you, Johnnie," she said. "Anything."

"Okay," he said. "Help me get some of these guns packed and out of here."

Later, they stood on the sidewalk with the rest of the

gang, watching as the firemen chopped through the roof, sending bright sparks flying into the black night.

They were all fully dressed, and the men were armed with automatics and shoulder holsters, but most of their luggage had to be left behind in the burning hotel, including four machine guns, and three steel vests in special cases. There were also rifles and shotguns and pistols, the dismantled parts hidden between tailor-made suits and perfumed lingerie.

Evelyn held tightly to Dillinger's arm, her gray eyes wide and loving as she looked up at him. "Let's get out of here, Johnnie," she whispered.

"In a minute. I've got to get those guns out of there."

"Forget 'em, Johnnie. It's not worth taking the chance."

"Look, honey. We need those guns." He called out to Pierpont and Makley. "Try to get a couple of those firemen to carry down the bags," he said. "Give them a sawbuck or something."

"We've tried," Makley said. "They're still trying to get people out of the damn place."

"We'd better get out of here before they spot those rods," Pierpont said. "I think we oughta take off for California tonight."

Dillinger shook his head. "You guys get rooms somewhere. We'll meet tomorrow night in the parking lot at the Marimar Club. Ten o'clock sharp."

For the second time in a little over two months, Dillinger was caught napping. This time it was on the living room sofa of his new furnished apartment in Tucson. Evelyn was on the sofa with him, her head on his bare chest, her lips moving on his breast as she slept.

"Cozy," said a plainclothes cop in a white sombrero and handmade boots. He was a big man with skin like dry leather and eyes as blue as an Arizona sky. "I feel like a meanie waking him up."

Three husky troopers surrounded the sofa, waiting for the officer in the white sombrero to give the command before pouncing on the sleeping man and woman.

"He's a good sleeper," White Sombrero said, tipping

83

back the hat. "Let's see what kind of nerves he's got."
Grinning mischievously he leaned over, his mouth next to
the sleeping man's ear.

"Hey, Dillinger!" he shouted, his voice blasting like a
trumpet.

Dillinger shot up so quickly his head struck against
White Sombrero's chin, knocking him halfway across the
room. Evelyn flew off the sofa, landing on her stomach.
In the next instant, Dillinger was up and dashing wildly
for the door. The trooper nearest him, an ex-All-State football star, sailed through the air, his powerful shoulder
cutting Dillinger just below the knees, folding him like a
jackknife.

White Sombrero, holding his bleeding chin in his hand,
quickly stepped forward and pulled Dillinger up from the
floor.

"Nervous character, aren't you?" he said.

"Dirty screw," Dillinger growled, jerking his arm out
of the trooper's grip.

"Just don't try to go anywhere," White Sombrero said.
"Get your clothes on and don't give us any trouble. Understand?"

Dillinger's hands clenched into hard fists.

"Johnnie, don't," Evelyn sobbed from the floor. "Please
do what he says."

"You okay, baby?" he asked, his face relaxing. "The
bastards are jealous. Who ever heard of them. I'm John
Dillinger. Who are they?"

White Sombrero nodded to one of the troopers. "Get
this bum in there and dress him up."

"Don't touch me," Dillinger said, side-stepping the
trooper.

"Then get some duds on and no more foolin' around."

Scowling angrily, Dillinger went into the bedroom,
followed by two troopers.

"You too, lady," White Sombrero said. "Get with it."

Leaning against the sofa, he took out his handkerchief
and carefully mopped his bleeding chin. "Wonder what the
fuss is all about, anyway," he said in a half whisper. "Seems
to me like a lot of whoopin' and hollerin' for nothing."

The roundup netted the Arizona police four desperadoes—Dillinger, Makley, Pierpont and Clark—three gun molls—Evelyn, Opal Long and Mary Kinder—and enough armament to start a first-class South American revolution.

White Sombrero had more to say to the press. The police work had been relatively simple. Tipped off by firemen on the night of the hotel fire, they had found guns and other articles of gang warfare in four rooms. Hotel employees had then positively identified mug shots of all four outlaws. From there it had been a routine matter of checking all hotels, apartment and rooming houses, which had taken them less than three days. The arrests themselves had come off without a hitch.

Louis Piquett shook his head, the two-inch shock of white hair trembling impatiently. "Johnnie, there are four states fighting over you right now. Can't you get that straight through your head? You're in serious trouble. Very serious trouble. They've got a murder rap hanging over you in Indiana. That's a capital offense."

"Sit down," Dillinger said. "You make me nervous."

"Well, I hope so," Piquett said. "I'm glad to hear that something makes you nervous. For a while there I didn't think it was possible."

"Louie, they haven't built a jail strong enough to hold John Dillinger. You just do what I tell you, the same as last time. Play for time. Delay all you can. I'll find a way out."

"Well, for God's sake, don't tell them about it."

"Why not?"

"Play it smart, Johnnie. Be friendly with everybody. Act like you're sorry about everything and you're going to repent."

Dillinger pulled on his lower lip. "Yeah, I'll buy that. Get 'em off guard. I see what you mean."

"Right now they've got a company of national guardsmen protecting this jail. Nobody could break out."

Dillinger laughed, remembering the events of the last two days. "Hey, didn't I play it smart with that prosecutor? See my picture in the paper—the two of us shaking hands like a couple of old pals? You should have seen the look in his eyes. It was like he was seeing the devil for the first time. Even the reporters. They're all very impressed with me. Like a movie star, you know. Hell, the governor, the attorney general, all the big shots have been down here gaping at me. It's very funny."

"Well, Johnnie, it's natural. You're a very colorful character."

Dillinger shrugged. "There must be more than that to it."

Piquett sat down on the bunk next to him. "It is more than that, Johnnie. You're sort of a hero in a way. Especially to the poor people, the ones who are getting it in the neck right now. No food or coal or even a decent roof over their heads. They feel beaten and discouraged and they don't know what to do about it. Then they read about you and for a brief moment they become you. They are brave and strong and brutal, robbing banks and shooting policemen, riding away in a big fast car with a real looker at their side.

"It's escape, Johnnie. Escape from the dreary, meaningless round of everyday living. They're frightened and they're also bored. You represent everything they are not and everything they secretly desire to be. You're like Nick Carter, except you're better than Nick Carter. You're not tied down by ethics or scruples or principles. You're the devil hidden in every man's soul, the beast locked in every hungry heart."

"I don't get it," he said. "Who's a beast?"

"Johnnie, Johnnie. All I'm saying is that you actually do the things other people only think about."

"You mean I'm a man of action?" Dillinger said, trying to capture the gist of Piquett's meaning.

"Something like that, Johnnie."

"Well, that's what I believe in. Don't just think about something. Do it. When you think about it chances are you'll never do it."

"We're living in strange times," Piquett said. "Very strange."

"You're no angel," Dillinger said.

Piquett stood up. "That I'm not, Johnnie. Fortunately, there are very few around nowadays."

The next day, shackled to Makley, Pierpont and Clark, Dillinger was ushered into court and promptly arraigned. Newsmen and photographers crowded around the prisoners, shouting their questions at a smiling Dillinger, who parried loaded questions as deftly as a Southern politician.

"Bum rap," he said, referring to the O'Malley slaying. "I was in Miami at the time. Been in the South a whole month."

Cameras popped in his face, the white flash blinding him, but he continued to smile.

"They ain't got nothing on me," he said. "Nothing at all. You guys made it all up in your stories."

"Hey, come on, Johnnie," one newsman protested. "Level with us. We've been good to you. Give us a break."

Dillinger shook his head. "You guys and these cops are framing me. I'm clean."

Even the troopers laughed at this one. White Sombrero walked in front of Dillinger, a cigar clenched in his strong white teeth. "Don't insult Mr. Dillinger, boys," he said. "He's a very sensitive man."

Inside the courtroom, Dillinger sat at a long table with the other three prisoners. Behind them troopers stood stiffly at attention, their machine guns at half-mast. Dillinger listened closely when Piquett addressed the court, but otherwise seemed uninterested. Bail was set at $400,000. The four prisoners looked at each other and shrugged apathetically.

They were led back to the jail and locked in their cells. Suddenly, Dillinger whirled about, grabbing the bars tightly. "You can't keep me in any two-by-four jail like this," he shouted. "I'll get out and kill you all." He shook his fist at the officers and reporters, his yellow eyes flashing murderously.

On the evening of January 29, with hands and legs shackled, Dillinger was thrown into the back seat of a black limousine and whisked to the airport. There, accompanied

87

by four burly detectives, he was dragged, cursing and kicking, from the car and forced inside a two-engine plane. It was his first airplane ride. After a stop in Douglas, Arizona, the plane headed for Chicago, where it landed at six-ten the next evening.

Coatless and hatless, shivering in his thin blue suit, Dillinger was half dragged and half carried down the aluminum ladder. Newsreel cameramen, newspaper photographers and scores of reporters fought to get close to the prisoner, who was roughly pushed through the crowd, his arm folded across his face to shield his eyes from the white glare of floodlights and flash bulbs. One hundred and seventeen policemen, most of them armed with submachine guns and protected by bulletproof vests, formed a cordon, closing out the entire area to unauthorized personnel.

With Dillinger at his side, Lieutenant Frank Reynolds stopped before one of the black limousines and addressed the newsmen. "I have orders," he said, glancing at Dillinger, "to kill the prisoner if any attempt is made to rescue him."

"Lieutenant," one of the newsmen asked. "How do you intend to do that?"

"I will shoot him," Reynolds said flatly.

Dillinger seemed unimpressed by the statement.

"Mr. Dillinger," another newsman asked, "where is John Hamilton?"

"Dead," Dillinger said. "He died in Miami when we were there on vacation."

"You mean, Mr. Dillinger, that Hamilton was not with you in East Chicago on January 15th?"

"We were all in Miami," Dillinger said. "I had nothing to do with that job. This is a lousy frame-up."

"That's enough," Reynolds said.

"Have a heart, Lieutenant. Just a couple more questions?"

"No more, boys. We've got a long ride ahead of us."

The ride from Chicago to Crown Point, Indiana, was about fifty miles. Eight police cars, loaded down with forty-five officers, escorted by a dozen motorcycle cops, made the trip to Crown Point that evening. Sirens wailed and flags waved on the front of the official cars. Policemen sat tensely inside the big cars, their fingers stiff on their weapons, their eyes staring sharply out into the darkness.

Dillinger sat next to Lieutenant Reynolds, a mocking grin on his relaxed face, pleased by all the attention. "I appreciate all this service," he said. "I used to have me a car like this, but I didn't have any siren or flag. It's very nice."

"Want a cigarette?" Reynolds asked.

"Wouldn't have a cigar on you, would you?"

"Don't smoke 'em."

"Too bad," Dillinger said. "It's a pretty good habit." He took the cigarette and Reynolds lit it with his silver lighter.

"Have any trouble in Tucson?" Reynolds asked.

Dillinger shrugged. "The usual crap. Show me a screw and I'll show you a sadist."

"A what?"

"A sadist. Louie says that's a guy who gets kicks from beating others."

"Yeah, I know," Reynolds said. "I'm just surprised you know."

"What do you think I am?" Dillinger asked angrily. "A dummy or something?"

"You don't strike me as being overly bright," Reynolds said.

Dillinger's eyes narrowed. "You jerks are all the same," he said. "You think you're the only guys who know anything."

"How bright can you be," Reynolds said, "and do the things you do? No, I'd say you're pretty stupid."

Dillinger's mouth opened, then closed tightly, the muscles along the ridge of his strong jaw bulging out against his smooth cheeks. He shrugged and turned his head to look out the window. "Have it your way," he said. "Who cares what a lousy screw thinks anyway?"

CHAPTER NINE

Sheriff Lillian Holley was a law enforcement officer of a different gender. She had succeeded to the title by default. Her husband, the elected sheriff of Lake County, had been killed by a berserk farmer. According to Indiana custom, Lillian Holley had been appointed to complete her husband's term of office.

Dillinger's first look at Sheriff Holley visibly shook him. She stomped down the jailhouse steps, decked out in fringed buckskin skirt and vest, plaid shirt with white kerchief knotted under her wattled chin, thick ankles stuffed into black leather boots, and wide hips spilling over the silver-studded gun belt and pearl-handled six-shooter. Her round freckled face beamed at him from under the white Stetson.

"Howdy, Johnnie," she said, pumping his hand manfully. "I'm the sheriff around these here parts. Holley's the name."

Dillinger shot a perplexed glance at Lieutenant Reynolds. "Glad to make your acquaintance, ma'am," he mumbled.

She laughed, squeezed his arm and pulled him up the steps into the jailhouse.

Newsmen gaped speechlessly.

Dillinger spent a month and three days in the Crown Point jail. In that time, he met every important official in the State of Indiana. He had his picture taken with his arm draped across the shoulder of County Prosecutor Robert Estill and another one smiling pleasantly at Sheriff Holley, who willingly returned the courtesy.

He stood in a line-up and was identified by seventeen customers and bank employees of the East Chicago First National, including Vice-President Spencer. He was arraigned, indicted and the murder trial was promptly set for February 13, and then, just as promptly, postponed to March 12.

Makley, Pierpont and Clark were transferred from Tucson to the Lima, Ohio jail to await trial for the murder of Sheriff Sarber. The three women were held for questioning and then released for lack of evidence.

Sheriff Holley had a motherly concern for her charges. She visited each cell daily, talking and joking with the prisoners, sometimes interjecting a little advice when she thought it was needed.

Dillinger's cell mate was Herbert Youngblood, a Negro awaiting trial for murder. At first Dillinger had resented Youngblood, interpreting the sheriff's action as a personal affront to him. It was an attempt to degrade him, he told Piquett. "They're trying to make me look like a two-bit punk."

On the other hand, Youngblood was proud of his partner. He sat on his bunk, his dark eyes fixed on Dillinger, studying his every movement.

"Hey, Mistah Dillinger," he asked one night. "You don't like nigras?"

Dillinger lay in his bunk, a cigarette dangling from his lips. He turned his head, his yellow eyes closely appraising the deeply wrinkled, dark face.

"I don't know," he said. "I never gave it much thought."

"I heard you talkin' the other day," Youngblood said. "I know."

"Oh, that," Dillinger said. "It ain't got nothing to do with you. A man with my reputation should get a private cell. I shouldn't be put with no bohunk, black or white."

"I'm a real bad man," Youngblood said. "I'm no bohunk."

Dillinger sat up, grinning. "How bad are you?" he asked.

"Real bad. I'm a killer."

Dillinger laughed and tossed his cigarette butt at him. Youngblood's hand shot up, snagged it in midair, and popped it into his mouth in one smooth catlike movement. He puffed, his large dark eyes gleaming proudly.

A few days later, Dillinger caught Youngblood with a pocketknife in his hand. "Where did ya get that?" he asked, reaching out for it.

"I sneaked it in," he said, moving away.

"Give it here," Dillinger said, stalking him around the cell.

"It's mine," he said. "I'm gonna stick me somebody with it." He lashed out quickly, his eyes flashing, the blade barely missing Dillinger's throat.

Dillinger's eyes narrowed, but he didn't move back. "Put it here," he said, reaching out, palm up. "Nice and easy."

Youngblood made another pass. This time the blade actually flicked against the loose flesh under his chin. "This is your last chance, black boy," he said. "Put it here or else."

Youngblood's eyes flashed again but this time his hand remained at his side. A moment later he was laughing, shaking his large head. "Hot damn, if that don't beat everythin'. And me being such a bad man and all. I nearly killed me John Dillinger. Hot damn."

"Right here," Dillinger said, pointing to his palm. "Nice and easy."

Shaking all over with laughter, Youngblood placed the knife in his palm. "You got nerves, Mr. Dillinger. Yes, sir. Real bad man nerves."

"I've got a knife," Dillinger said.

"Yes, sir. That you sure do."

"And I've got me a way out of this tin can."

"Ooops," Youngblood said, leaning up close. "I's listenin'."

Dillinger ran his thumb across the sharp edge of the blade. "I've got me a knife and I've got me a brain," he said. "That's all a man needs to make himself a key."

Eight days later blaring headlines told of John Dillinger's use of the key:

DILLINGER ESCAPES AGAIN
USES WOODEN PISTOL
LOCKS GUARDS IN CELL

CROWN POINT, Ind., March 4—John Dillinger, notorious bank robber and murderer, walked out of the heavily guarded and supposedly escape-proof Lake County jail this morning in a daring escape that rivals the exploits of the heroes of Wild West thrillers.

In the course of his record-making break he locked thirty-three persons in cells or storerooms. From them he forced contributions of $15 for expenses.

He cowed his guards, locking them and thirteen fellow prisoners in a single cell, after threatening them with a two-ounce piece of wood which he had whittled to resemble a pistol and which he had stained with shoe blacking.

Then, with a Negro murderer, Herbert Youngblood, he helped himself to two of the jail's machine guns and walked to a nearby garage in search of an automobile. There Dillinger and Youngblood overawed half a dozen employees, stole the automobile of Sheriff Lillian Holley and drove away, taking with them Deputy Sheriff Ernest Blunk, the jail's fingerprint expert, and Edward Saagers, a garageman, as hostages.

HUNTED BY AN ARMY

Having made good his boast that he would escape any jail, Dillinger was being hunted tonight by an army of law officials. One of them was Mrs. Holley, Lake County's sheriff.

"If I ever see John Dillinger I'll shoot him through the head with my own pistol," the woman sheriff exclaimed. She had declared Dillinger would never escape from her custody.

The desperado was believed to be somewhere in the Chicago countryside tonight. Police of the city were notified to be on the alert and to shoot to kill if they saw him. The Indiana State Police also were mobilized to scour the countryside for him.

Dillinger had been here since Jan. 30 for trial March 12 on a charge of shooting and killing Policeman William Patrick O'Malley in the $20,000 holdup of the First National Bank of East Chicago on Jan. 15. He and three members of his gang, Harry Pierpont, Russell Clark and Charles Makley, had been arrested Jan. 26 at Tucson, Ariz. Seventeen witnesses had identified Dillinger and the state prosecuting authorities were certain that he would be sent to the electric chair.

In his comparatively brief stay in the Lake County Jail the all-around "bad man" had come to be known among his fellow prisoners as "John the Whittler." His seemingly harmless pastime of playing with a piece of wood and a knife was a matter of amusement to the guards and to the other inmates of the jail. Where he got the knife was not learned.

None suspected that the hobby was part of a cunning plot to effect a jail break. Guffaws greeted Dillinger whenever he boasted to fellow inmates, "I'm going to shoot my way out of this."

The bravado of this latest escape of the resourceful defier of prison bars, once an Indiana farm boy, was typical of his career. He is accused by the police of having robbed more than 100 banks.

Dillinger's first step in his almost incredible feat came about 8:30 A.M. when Blunk entered the cell occupied by Henry Jelinek and the bank robber to obtain fingerprints of the former, who is held on a murder charge.

Blunk was unarmed. Dillinger thrust the blackened toy pistol, which looked like the real thing, against the deputy sheriff's ribs and commanded him to hurry into a bull-pen cell. Meekly, the deputy sheriff obeyed and the cell door clanged behind him.

A minute or two later Warden Louis Baker entered the cell. He, too, was frightened into surrender by the wooden pistol. Hardly had the warden been shoved into the cell beside Blunk when the turnkey, Sam Calhoon, chanced on the scene. In one arm he held a bundle of soap for his charges. In the other hand were the keys of the jail. Also terrified by the bogus weapon, Calhoon yielded the keys to Dillinger and was shoved into captivity with Blunk and Baker.

Turning then to thirteen of his fellow prisoners, Dillinger snapped:

"Now, you guys get in with them."

The convicts, some of them chuckling at what they considered a joke, obeyed. The lock of the bull pen turned on them. Dillinger had accomplished his first step.

SEIZES MACHINE GUNS

Moving carefully for fear of awaking the deputy sheriff, Ernest Baar, who was off duty and who had decided to rest in a place where he would be "ready if there was any trouble," slumbered on.

Dillinger descended to the first floor, and entered the jail office, in which sat an Indiana National Guardsman, Warden Hiles. Hiles, presumably, was helping to keep Dillinger from getting out of jail.

The guardsman did not see the bandit slip into the office and take two loaded machine guns, resting on a table in a small booth. Before the guardsman realized it, Dillinger was pointing one of the machine guns at him.

Without further ado, Dillinger forced the militiaman to walk upstairs and enter the bull pen with the other victims.

Then he spoke to Youngblood and Jelinek.

"You two can go with me," he said.

"Yes, sir," said Youngblood.

"I don't want any part of your business," demurred Jelinek. "You go your way. I like it better here."

"Okay," answered Dillinger.

He handed one of the machine guns to. Youngblood and ordered Blunk to come out of the cell. The deputy obeyed and Dillinger locked the door on the other captives.

JEERS AT CAPTIVES IN PEN

Then, standing in the corridor, Dillinger surveyed the inmates of the bull pen.

"Ha! Ha! Ha!" he roared. "The joke is on you jerks. I did it with my little wooden pistol."

With the helpless Blunk in the lead, Dillinger and Youngblood went to the jail kitchen, where the matron, Mrs. Lou Linton, was bustling about with her breakfast duties.

"Just be a good girl," said Dillinger. "If you keep quiet, nothing will happen to you."

Mrs. Linton made the promise, and kept it.

With their guns trained on Blunk, the fugitives went through the hall yard into an alley and then to a basement, in which stood two automobiles. Unable to start the motor of either machine, they went through the alley and out of the jail, passing the Lake County Criminal Court Building, in which Dillinger was to have stood trial.

While crossing the street, Dillinger spotted a national guardsman and two deputy sheriffs standing half a block away. He walked up to them, pulled the machine gun from under his jacket which he carried on his arm and said, "Come on, boys." He took them into the jail and locked them up.

Still accompanied by Youngblood and Blunk, he went out the rear entrance of the jail and casually crossed the street to the Main Street Garage, about 150 yards from the jail. A few moments later, the trio entered the garage by a side door.

In the garage were Saagers, several other employes and Robert Volk, a mail carrier, who carried a pistol. Volk, however, had removed his belt and the weapon was slung over his shoulder. He made no move to shoot, and Dillinger, letting Youngblood do the guarding, turned to Saagers.

95

OFF IN THE SHERIFF'S CAR

"What's the fastest car in the place?" he demanded.

Saagers guessed that the sheriff's machine was the best. It was a Ford V-8, bearing Indiana license 679-929 and had a red headlight.

Dillinger took it. He shoved Blunk into the driver's seat, ordered Saagers and Youngblood into the rear seat, climbed into the machine and issued orders to Blunk.

"Drive slow and easy. Forty miles an hour is plenty."

The car started away, going north. Avoiding the traveled roads and taking gravel bypaths, the fugitives and their prisoners reached a point about twenty miles east of Peotone, where the machine skidded on the muddy road and toppled into a ditch.

Saagers related later that forty minutes elapsed before the car was pulled back to the road and chains were put on the wheels to prevent further mishaps of such a nature. Dillinger endured the enforced halt patiently.

The car finally righted, the party resumed their flight, driving toward Peotone, still not exceeding the forty-mile-an-hour speed. About four miles east of Peotone, Dillinger began looking around.

"This looks like a forlorn neighborhood," he said. "No telephone wires anywhere. Pull it up."

Blunk stopped the car and they all got out. "This is as far as you go, boys. This colored boy and me will take it up from here." He gave Saagers a cigarette and four dollars, which he said was carfare back to Crown Point. After shaking hands with the two hostages, he told Youngblood to get in the rear seat and they sped away, with Dillinger singing, "I'm heading for the last roundup . . ."

Saagers telephoned from a farmhouse to the authorities and made his way in company with Blunk into Peotone. There they said that Dillinger seemed to be in a high good humor and was especially pleased with himself for hoodwinking his guards with a wooden pistol.

SHERIFF PROMPT IN PURSUIT

Mrs. Holley, furious at the escape, lost no time in starting pursuit. The moment she learned of the break she telephoned to the police at nearby Gary, Ind., shouting over the wire:

"Send all the police and guns you've got. Dillinger's loose."

Her chagrin at the escape was in no way lessened by the comment of Governor Paul V. McNutt.

"We offered to take Dillinger to the penitentiary and Sheriff Holley declined," said the governor. "We have begun our investigation to determine the reasons for the refusal as well as of the other factors in the case."

Earlier in the week, Mrs. Holley had told newsmen, "He may be able to fight his way out of some jails, but he won't break this jail. We brought out machine guns when we heard he was captured. Every day the deputies have been practicing. I have little fear of anything short of an army."

Immediately upon hearing of Dillinger's escape, officials at the Lima, Ohio jail began converting the courthouse grounds into an armed carmp.

Sandbag barricades were thrown up about the prison where the Dillinger henchmen, Harry Pierpont, Charles Makley and Russell Clark are awaiting trial for first degree murder in the killing of Sheriff Jesse Sarber on Oct. 12, when they rescued Dillinger from the same cell they are now occupying.

The three henchmen, dressed in pajamas, were lounging in the sheriff's office when they heard the radio announcement of Dillinger's escape. Jumping up, the pajama-clad prisoners dashed to their cells, put on their best suits, and waited for Dillinger to come along and free them.

Attorney Louis Piquett, in a statement to the press, said Dillinger suffered from claustrophobia, a dread of confined spaces. Therefore, he did not like staying in jails.

John Stege, supervising captain of the Chicago police, was quoted as predicting Dillinger could be expected to gather up his gang, raid an armory or a police station to obtain weapons and "rob a bank first thing on Monday morning."

It was one of Dillinger's boasts that he could "go through a bank" and take all the money out of it in three minutes and forty seconds.

Speaking to newsmen in Peotone, Edwin Saagers pointed out that John Dillinger was the coldest and toughest criminal alive. "I have just finished riding more than fifty miles with him;" he said. "And it was the most exciting ride of my life."

CHAPTER TEN

In the Builders' Building in Chicago, Louis Piquett listened to the continuous police progress report on the radio. His white hair stood straight up on his head and his small black marble eyes were excited as he looked at the people gathered around him: Evelyn Frechette, Marie Conforti, Homer Van Meter, Jack Hamilton, Helen Gillis and her husband, Lester, better known in the press as "Baby Face" Nelson.

Newspapers were scattered about the floor with empty coffee containers and sandwich wrappers. Dillinger had been out nearly fourteen hours and still he had not con-tacted them.

"Something's wrong," Evelyn repeated. "I can feel it. He's hurt, maybe lying somewhere, bleeding to death."

Piquett shook his head. "Not Johnnie," he said. "He's okay. That boy leads a charmed life."

"Oh, I wish I could believe you," Evelyn said.

"Believe me," Piquett said. "I mean every word of it."

"He's right," Hamilton said. "Johnnie's got a rabbit's foot in each fist and two in every pocket. He'll call when he gets a chance. Don't worry."

Homer sat on the edge of his chair, his moist eyes glistening with excitement. Marie was stretched out on a leather couch, trying to sleep. Nelson paced up and down the office, stopping every time a new announcement came over the radio. Helen sat next to Evelyn, smoking calmly, a bored look on her dark face.

"Jesus," Baby Face said. "The heat's really on now."

"He's the most wanted man in the world," Piquett said. "Now even the G-men are after him."

"Why the G-men?" Homer asked.

98

"Transporting a stolen car over a state line," Piquett said. "It's a violation of the Dyer Act. A federal rap."

"What's the diff?" Baby Face said. "Cops are cops."

"Plenty," Piquett said. "Those boys never let up once they get on a case like this. And they don't have to worry about state lines. They can go anywhere and make arrests."

"They've got to catch you first," Baby Face said, grinning coldly, his boyish freckled face belying even his twenty-six years.

Hamilton's dark piercing eyes were studying him from across the room. Just a kid, he thought. Just a lousy runty kid except for that look in his ice-blue eyes. And that was all you had to see to understand why he had become so feared by cops and desperadoes alike.

Next to Dillinger and "Pretty Boy" Floyd, he was the most wanted man in the country. And in some ways, the most dangerous. Some fellows said he was kill-crazy, that he liked nothing better than killing cops. They said that he actually waited on the highway for a police car so he could give chase and mow 'em down with his chopper, laughing like Harry Pierpont had laughed the night he had killed that cop in the alley behind the Beverly Gardens.

Hamilton wondered why Dillinger had personally requested Piquett to get in touch with Baby Face. Sure, they needed a new gang now, but he had already recruited three men, Joe Burns, Eddie Green and Tommy Carroll, all guys they had known in stir. All good men, too. Maybe not as good as Pierpont, Clark or Makley, but good enough, with plenty of guts and savvy. And they wouldn't give a man trouble. Which was more than he could say for Nelson.

The call came early the next morning. Piquett, his face tense, his eyes staring into space, listened to Dillinger's voice, nodding, hardly saying a word.

"Okay, Johnnie," he said, finally. "I'll see what I can do. Evelyn will give you the word when she sees you tonight. Good luck, boy." He listened some more. "Yeah. I understand. Don't worry. Jack's fine. He's here right now. Want to talk to him? All right. I'll tell him. 'Bye. Take care of yourself."

He hung up and passed a nervous hand through his white hair. "What a man," he said. "I never met anybody like him."

"Damnit," Evelyn said. "What did he say?"

"He's in Chicago," Piquett said. "He'll meet you tonight at the corner of Wells and Erie, ten o'clock sharp. Have a car and take Jack along."

"How about me?" Homer said. "Didn't he say nothing about me?"

Piquett shook his head. "He was in a hurry."

"Where is he staying?" Nelson asked.

"I don't know. But, Evelyn, he needs a place. I thought maybe Ana could fix him up. She's got a basement room in that place of hers on Dearborn. I used it for a client once. Why don't you arrange it? The old rooming house on Halsted is out now. Too hot."

"God Almighty," Homer said. "Nobody, but nobody, can stop Johnnie Dillinger."

Piquett shook his head. I'm afraid a lot of people are trying to do just that right now. It can't go on much longer. No, I'd say John Dillinger has reached his peak. From now on it's all going to be downhill. And it's going to be one hell of a fast ride."

The bank robbery predicted by Captain John Stege in the newspaper did not take place on Monday morning following Dillinger's escape.

It was Tuesday morning. And six hundred miles from Chicago.

Sioux Falls, situated in the southeastern part of South Dakota, ten miles from the Minnesota state line, was a city of some 25,000 population in 1934. At ten o'clock on the morning of March 6, a large black sedan pulled up in front of the First National Bank. Two policemen, standing before the bank entrance, casually observed its arrival and continued their animated conversation.

A moment later John Dillinger swung out of the sedan, a machine gun in his hands.

"Hey, you coppers," he called. "Freeze!"

Behind him five men jumped out of the sedan, each

holding a machine gun. Baby Face Nelson walked past Dillinger and up to the two policemen.

"I'll take care of these monkeys," he said.

"There's a good place," Dillinger said, pointing across the street with the muzzle of the gun. "With your back against that brick wall nobody can get to you."

Grinning, Nelson crossed the street with the two policemen beside him. Dillinger waited until he was stationed, then hurried into the bank with the other men following him.

A crowd had begun to gather on the sidewalk by this time. Still grinning diabolically, Nelson waved the chopper at them. "Get back or I'll blow the daylight out of you," he yelled.

Inside the bank, Hamilton and Dillinger had taken positions in the middle of the lobby while the three new men, Eddie Green, Joe Burns and Tommy Carroll, quickly emptied the tellers' cages and vault.

"Get all of it," Dillinger shouted.

Suddenly, there was the loud stutter of a machine gun and Dillinger smiled crookedly at Hamilton. "I guess Baby Face is showing them who's boss," he said.

Hamilton did not answer. His piercing black eyes stayed fixed on the group of clerks and bank officials lined up against a wall.

"What's the matter?" Dillinger asked.

"He's crazy," Hamilton said. "He's out of his goddamn head."

Dillinger gave a short laugh. "So who cares? He's tough, ain't he? That's the kind of boys I need. The tougher the better. From now on everybody's gonna have to be real tough."

Hamilton nodded. "Can you see the crowd out there?"

"Don't worry about it."

"Yeah. I'll bet the cops are on the roofs right now, waiting to pick us off when we come out."

Carroll came running out with Burns and Green behind him. "Clean as a whistle," he said.

"Burns, Green," Dillinger said. "Grab four of those dames over there and bring 'em out here."

101

They came out of the bank with the four girls held before them as shields. Baby Face was already running toward them.

"Look at that crowd," he cried. "Must be at least a thousand people here."

"My friends," Dillinger said, suddenly waving to them.

Catcalls, loud whistles and some applause greeted the gesture.

"Let's get out of here," Hamilton said, jumping into the car.

Waving once more, Dillinger climbed into the car, followed by the other men. The four girls, hysterical and crying, were pulled to the running board and held there as the black sedan sped away. Eight miles out of town, the car stopped and the four girls were released.

"Thanks, girls," Dillinger said. "You were a great help."

The men laughed and Homer drove off.

"You just made them famous," Tommy Carroll said. "They'll get their puss in the paper and everything. Might even become movie stars."

"I had a thousand people out there," Nelson said. "And a dozen coppers. Even the chief of police. He came running up there and I burned a couple slugs over his head, just high enough for him to hear them sing. He fell back in line real quick."

In St. Paul that evening, they counted the swag which amounted to $46,000. Dillinger took his usual twenty-five per cent cut off the top and the others split the rest into six equal parts.

"I've gotta have a bigger cut," Nelson said afterwards, scowling unhappily. "That job was my idea."

Dillinger was stretched out on a sofa, with his legs drawn up over the back of it. There was a cigarette in his mouth and a drink in his hand. Evelyn sat on the sofa, leaning against his legs. As usual, he had the two pistols under his armpits and the cartridge belt around his waist.

"Everybody gets the same cut," he said. "Except me."

Nelson walked up to the sofa and looked down at Dillinger. "I'm as famous as you are," he said. "I'm no dumb palooka."

"I don't have no dumb palookas working for me," Dillinger said, taking a pull on the drink. "They're all good boys."

"Don't make me laugh," Nelson said. "That stupid Van Meter couldn't rob a candy store by himself."

They were alone in the apartment with Evelyn and Nelson's wife, Helen.

"Homer's been with me a long time," he said.

"I don't care," Nelson said. "I say I get a bigger cut."

Dillinger pushed Evelyn away and swung his legs down and sat up on the sofa, his arms folded across his chest, his fingers touching the gun butts.

"I don't like arguments," he said, his narrowed eyes glinting ominously.

"You don't scare me," Nelson said. "I was knocking off banks long before you saw the inside of one."

There was a gentle knock at the door and Evelyn opened it to Hamilton. He stepped into the room and stopped, immediately aware of the tension between the two men. Slowly, his hand reached inside his suit jacket toward the holstered gun.

"What's up, Johnnie?" he asked, moving to the other side of the room, placing Nelson in a cross-fire position between himself and Dillinger.

"Nothing," Dillinger said.

Nelson glanced at Hamilton, then back at Dillinger, the diabolical grin back on his boyish face. "I'm worth it, Johnnie," he said.

"Yeah," Dillinger said. "I guess you are at that. From now on you get five per cent of my cut without nobody but us knowing it."

"Okay, that's more like it. Don't forget, until you broke jail I was worth more dough than you was on them posters."

"That was before," Dillinger said. "Now is now and that's what counts. Not before but now."

"That can change, too," Nelson said. "Changes come quick in this business. Who knows, one good break and I can be at the top of the list just like that." He snapped his fingers and gave a loud maniacal laugh, winking at his wife.

103

"Yeah, that's right," Dillinger said. "And one bad break and you can be at the bottom. Six feet under."

The next bank job was in Mason City, Iowa. The take was $52,344 and this time there were eight hostages crowding the car's running board when the bandits fled the town.

President Willis Bayley was shot through the door of his office as he tried to lock himself in, the slugs grazing his chest. He reeled out and collapsed in front of Nelson.

A uniformed guard, Tom Walters, seated in a bulletproof glass cage above the lobby, watched helplessly as machine gun bullets bounced off the glass enclosure. Due to the crowded conditions below him, he was unable to answer the fire. Later, he dropped a couple of gas bombs, but it was too late to do any good.

On March 11, Harry Pierpont and Charles Makley were convicted of first degree murder and sentenced to the electric chair. Russell Clark got life imprisonment.

On March 22, Herbert Youngblood shot it out with Port Huron, Michigan, police, killing one officer before falling mortally wounded. "I'm a bad man," he said, before dying. "A real bad man."

That same week, a columnist in the Chicago *Tribune* facetiously summed up the nationwide manhunt for Dillinger:

> Mr. Dillinger was seen yesterday looking over the new spring gloves in a State Street store in Chicago; negotiating for a twelve-cylinder car in Springfield, Illinois; buying a half dozen sassy cravats in Omaha, Nebraska; bargaining for a suburban bungalow at his home town of Mooresville, Indiana, and shaking hands with old friends; drinking a glass of soda water in a drugstore in Charleston, South Carolina; and strolling down Broadway swinging a Malacca cane in New York.
>
> He also bought a fishing rod in a sporting goods store in Montreal and gave a dinner at a hotel in Yucatan, Mexico. But, anyhow, Mr. Dillinger seems to have kept very carefully out of London, Berlin, Rome, Moscow, and Vienna. Or at least if he did go to those places yesterday he was traveling incog.

At the same time Chicagoans were chuckling over the

story of two automobiles, one with Indiana and one with Illinois plates, which spent hours chasing each other around the Windy City. When at last they met, out of each car bounded police, mutually convinced that the other automobile contained Dillinger.

A postal card mailed in St. Louis and signed John Dillinger was received in Lima, Ohio, warning the Ohio National Guard that he was on his way to release his three pals, recently convicted of murder.

Dillinger's sister in Mooresville received a letter from her brother which told her not to worry about him because that wouldn't help anything, "and besides, I'm having a lot of fun." Then, commenting on recent newspaper reports that he had used a real .45 automatic to break out of jail instead of the wooden gun, he said: "That's just a lot of hooey to cover up because they don't like to admit that I locked eight deputies and a dozen trusties up with my wooden gun before I got my hands on the two machine guns and you should have seen their faces. Ha! Ha! Ha! Pulling that off was worth ten years of my life. Ha! Ha!"

A London newspaper told its readers that even Red Indians were after Dillinger. They had taken to the war-path, hunting the desperado with bows and arrows.

In Crown Point, Indiana, a special grand jury began an investigation of Sheriff Holley's office and all jail personnel in an attempt to fix responsibility for Dillinger's escape.

Dillinger and Evelyn lived for nearly four weeks on the third floor of a modern apartment house in an exclusive section of St. Paul. They lived alone and quietly, rarely going out except to a movie.

There was a well-equipped kitchen and Evelyn cooked roast beef and mashed potatoes with thick beef gravy. They played records, danced, and slept a great deal.

Baby Face and Helen were frequent visitors. Homer and Marie came up only when invited. Hamilton dropped in daily, usually in the afternoon, to discuss the latest rumors and future business.

At three o'clock on the afternoon of March 31, Evelyn was seated on the floor before the phonograph, listening to a new Al Jolson recording, demurely sipping a Tom Collins. Dillinger and Hamilton were on the sofa, discussing a proposed vacation in northern Wisconsin.

"It's called Little Bohemia," Hamilton was saying. "It's way upstate, right on a lake. Big fir trees all around and plenty of hunting and fishing."

"Damn, that sounds good to me. Can we fix it up with the owner?"

Hamilton shook his head. "I don't think so. But so what. Hell, it'll be out of season. There'll be nobody there but us. We can take care of the owner."

"Let's bring the whole gang," Dillinger said. "In case something breaks, we'll have plenty of guns to fight our way out. Where did you hear about the place?"

"Some bartender at Fox River Grove. Used to go there every summer with his family."

There was a light tapping at the door and Dillinger nodded casually at Evelyn. "Get that, baby, will ya? It's probably Baby Face and Helen."

"Oh, damn," Evelyn said, "can't they stay home once in a while?"

As she walked by, Dillinger slapped her buttocks, grinning at Hamilton. "When you gonna get yourself a dame, Jackie?"

"I've got all the dames I need," he said. "Why buy a cow when milk is so cheap."

"It's not the same," Dillinger said. "That quick tussle with a dame is no good. This is the way to get it, regular and steady."

"It's the cops," Evelyn screamed, slamming the door and sliding the bolt.

"Out of the way," Dillinger shouted, both pistols suddenly in his hand and aimed at the door. Evelyn jumped back and he opened fire. "Get the choppers, Jack."

Hamilton ran into the bedroom, coming out with two submachine guns. "They're not shooting," he said. "I wonder how many of those bastards are out there?"

Dillinger took one of the machine guns, replacing the pistols in their holsters. "Take a gander out back."

He stood before the door, sending short bursts crashing

through the splintered wood. "Well, for Christ's sake," he shouted. "How about it?"

"Nobody, as far as I can see," Hamilton said.

"All right. You take Evelyn down the fire escape."

"How about you?" Evelyn cried.

"I'm going out the front," he said. "Jack, give me the keys to your car."

"No!" she screamed. "You come with us!"

"Go with Jack," he said coldly, catching the keys Hamilton had tossed to him from across the room. "No goddamn argument."

"Please, Johnnie, come with us."

"Take her, Jack. I'm getting out of here."

He fired another short burst and pulled the door open. A moment later he was standing in the middle of the hall-way, spraying lead in all directions. Then he ran headlong down the carpeted stairs, all three flights without stopping, and dashed out the front door, the gun blazing.

"Come on, you cowards," he shouted. "Show your heads."

The street was empty. He ran down the stone steps and along the sidewalk toward Hamilton's parked car. Suddenly, there was the sound of a pistol shot behind him and his left leg kicked out from under him. He went sprawling across the pavement, the machine gun clattering in front of him. He was up in a split second, whirling about, firing at two men who were running for cover. He emptied the drum and jumped into the car. His left leg felt completely paralyzed. He knew now that there was a slug in it, but he didn't have time to look at it. He twisted the key in the lock and the engine caught immediately. Slugs slapped against the car as he pulled away from the curb. Just as he turned the corner, he saw Eddie Green approaching from another direction, on his way to the apartment house.

"Sucker," he yelled. "Turn back."

Green did not see him. There was a smile on his face as he drove right into the police trap. Moments later he was dead.

The two federal agents and one local detective, who had been tipped off by a suspicious neighbor, broke into the empty apartment and found, besides the usual heavy armament, a snapshot of Dillinger, age 2, in a sailor suit, a glum expression on his face as he stared down at the camera from his perch atop a fence post. Next to the picture was a stack of news clippings describing his wooden-gun escape from the Crown Point jail.

Late that evening, Dr. Clayton E. May, of Minneapolis, fished out the slug from Dillinger's leg and dressed the wound. The desperado had lost a lot of blood and felt ill. That same night they drove back to Chicago. He lay on the back seat, wrapped in a blanket, and Evelyn sat on the floor holding a damp cloth against his fevered brow. Hamilton drove, taking all the back roads, the car bouncing in and out of ruts, shooting sharp pains into Dillinger's bandaged leg. He took the pain with gritted teeth, his eyes closed, his white face beaded with perspiration.

"Johnnie," Evelyn said softly. "Can you hear me?"

He nodded, his eyes still closed.

"I talked to Ana on the phone. She'll have that room ready for us when we get to Chicago."

He nodded, his eyes still closed.

"It's a pretty small room," she said. "But it'll be safe for the time being."

"How much?" Hamilton asked.

"Five hundred a week," Evelyn said.

Dillinger's eyes opened slightly. "The bitch!" he murmured.

"That's the way it is, Johnnie, when you're famous," Hamilton said. "It costs money. I know hideouts that cost a grand a week, and they're just filthy bug holes."

"I'll be okay in a couple of weeks," Dillinger said. "Then we'll go to that Little Bohemia in Wisconsin."

"Sure, Johnnie. That'll be great."

It was a damp, windowless basement room with two old army cots, a washstand, a chamber pot, a battered chest of drawers and one straight-back chair. There was no heat, no running water and no toilet.

For the first week, Dillinger stayed in bed under mounds of blankets, his yellow eyes appalled by the dreary surroundings.

Ana Sage came down once to collect the rent and to look at the feared desperado whose name made the headlines more often than the President of the United States.

"You ain't changed much since I last saw you on Halsted," she said. "Maybe a little more peaked."

From under the blankets, Dillinger glared balefully at her, but did not answer.

Evelyn nervously rearranged the blankets. "He feels much better now," she said. "He'll be up in no time."

Ana sat on the wooden chair and lit a cigarette. "If there's anything you need, just give the word."

"No, thank you," Evelyn said. "I'm gonna buy a little hot plate and cook our meals."

"It's gonna cost you extra for the electricity," she said.

Evelyn nodded. "I thought it would."

"Well, that's only fair, ain't it? After all, I'm taking a big chance with him down here."

"Yes," Evelyn said. "Yes, you are."

"And besides," she said. "He and his gang cost me a lot of good girls and never gave me nothing for it."

"We went because we wanted to," Evelyn said. "You didn't own us, you know."

"Opal and Mary are back," she said. "Maybe, you'll be back, too, someday."

Dillinger raised his head. "What's that supposed to mean?" he demanded.

Ana stood up. "I've got work to do," she said. "I can't spend all day gabbing down here." She wrinkled her nose. "It stinks down here. One of these days I'm gonna have this place cleaned up. Well, see ya later."

The next morning, Evelyn went shopping for the hot plate. Dillinger sat up in the bed to look at her. She was all dressed up, with a pert little black hat tilted to one side of her head, her curled hair soft against the other side of her face.

"Come here," he said, raising his arms.

"Now, Johnnie, don't mess me up." She leaned forward to be kissed.

His hand passed gently across her breasts and down her hips and buttocks to her thighs. "I like the feel of silk stockings," he said, running his hand up and down her leg.

"Don't like it too much," she said. "I've got to go."

"Me, too," he grinned.

"Johnnie, you be a good boy. I'll be right back."

His hand moved up along her thigh. "Just a minute," he said.

"No, Johnnie," she said, pushing his hand away. "I promise I'll be right back. Then you can feel my silk stockings all you want."

"Okay," he said. "Everything off but the silk stockings. Get some black ones."

"I've got some black ones," she said. "You ought to know."

"Get some real high ones, like the chorus girls wear."

"God, you're a character."

"Colorful," he said. "Don't forget that."

"Okay, you colorful character, I might even get some red ones that come way up to here."

"Okay," he said, lunging at her playfully.

She jumped back, blew him a kiss and quickly walked to the door. " 'Bye, 'bye, you horny little boy. I'll be right back."

He never saw her again.

Two hours later she was arrested by the Chicago police and turned over to the FBI. The charge was harboring a criminal and the sentence was two years in the Federal Detention Home at Milan, Michigan, plus a thousand-dollar fine.

CHAPTER ELEVEN

Emil Wanatka sat at a table before the large dining-room window overlooking the tree-lined entrance to his Little Bohemia Lodge. He was having his midmorning cup of coffee.

"It's turning warm, Mother," he said, smiling at his wife who sat across the table from him.

"Warmer than last year at this time," she observed. "There was ice on the lake till almost May last year."

"Well, it's about time we start fixing things up for the summer trade," he said. "Won't be long now."

Her eyes widened. "Emil, look out there."

"Well, I'll be doggoned," he said. "Looks like business already."

"Three cars full of people," she commented. "Do you suppose they're from Chicago?"

"Looks like Illinois plates," he said, getting to his feet. "I'd better go greet our guests."

Emil Wanatka stepped out and hurried to the three cars. A man with a small mustache and sunglasses climbed out of the first car and limped slowly toward Wanatka.

"Welcome to Little Bohemia Lodge, sir," Emile said, extending his hand in greeting.

The man ignored the hand and removed his sunglasses. "I'm John Dillinger," he said, matter-of-factly. "And these people are my friends."

Emil Wanatka stepped back apprehensively. "What do you want?"

"Nothing," Dillinger said. "A little hunting and fishing, and some rest."

"You can't stay here," Emil said. "You're criminals."

Dillinger smiled faintly. "Let me introduce my friends. All right, guys and girls, come over here. This is Jack

111

Hamilton, Homer Van Meter, Marie Conforti, Baby Face Nelson and his wife, Helen, John Paul Chase, Tommy Carroll and Jean Delaney. This little fella here is Pat Reilly who used to be mascot for the Minneapolis baseball team. The girl with him is Pat Cherrington. She's a dancer. You know, one of them strippers. What's your name?"

"Emil Wanatka."

"Well, Emil Wanatka, you be a good boy and nothing's gonna happen to you. If you're a wise guy, I'll kill you. Do you understand?"

Emil nodded gravely. "Yes, sir."

"Who's in there with you?"

"Just my wife. It's still out of season. We don't hire help till summer."

"That's fine. I see you've got a telephone."

"Yes, how did you know?"

Dillinger curved his thumb toward the telephone line. "Don't use it, old man. The first thing we'll do if the cops come barging in here is kill you and your wife. Don't forget it. I'm a man of my word."

"Yes, sir. How long are you and your friends planning to stay?"

"I don't know. Maybe a week, maybe forever. Who knows?" Suddenly, he burst out laughing and pounded Emil on the back. "Cheer up, this is gonna be fun."

Hamilton moved in front of Dillinger. "Okay, fellas, unload the cars and get them out of sight. Use the garages in the back."

"Remember this man," Dillinger told Wanatka, indicating Hamilton. "He takes good care of me. He thinks he's my mama."

Still laughing, Dillinger draped his arm around Wanatka's shoulder and pulled him toward the lodge. "Nice place you got here," he said. "I want the best rooms in the house for Jack and me. The rest of the gang can fight for what they get."

After lunch, Dillinger, Hamilton and Nelson took a stroll around the lodge. Two huge dogs came bounding out of the woods, barking angrily. Nelson jerked out his automatic and took careful aim.

Dillinger reached up and gripped his gun hand. "Don't be stupid," he said. "They're gonna be our watchdogs. Notice how they barked when we drove in here this morning? Well, they'll bark for cops, too."

The dogs stood a few feet away, growling fiercely. "Come here, boys," Dillinger said, slapping his thighs. "Come to papa. Come on, boys. There you are. Some more. Come. That's good, boys."

Both dogs sat before him, their tails wagging. He rubbed their heads and dug his fingers into their neck muscles. When he walked away, the dogs followed him eagerly.

"See these two barbed-wire fences on the right of the house?" Dillinger said. "That's fine. In case of attack, they'll have a hard time surrounding the house from this side. Especially if it's at night. Now let's check the other side of the house."

There were no barbed-wire fences on the left side, but there was a deep drainage ditch. "Not bad," Dillinger said. "If anybody comes from the front, we'll have plenty of time to get out the back."

"Let's take a look at that lake," Hamilton suggested.

Dillinger sat down on a tree stump. "That damn leg still bothers me," he said.

"That's nothing," Nelson said. "Want to see some real bullet holes? I can show you some corkers."

Dillinger frowned. "Who's this John Paul Chase?"

"Just a kid I met in Frisco after I broke pen in thirty-two."

"I don't like him," Dillinger said. "I don't like the way he keeps looking at me."

Nelson laughed. "I think he's in love with you," he said. "Talks about you all the time. I guess it's what they call hero worship."

"What good is he?"

"He's my business agent. You know—buys cars, guns, ammunition, makes contacts, finds hideouts, chauffeurs Helen around. He's my front man."

"Been on any jobs?"

"Not yet. He wants to, though."

"Yeah. Well, maybe we can take care of that."

113

"Might be gun-shy," Hamilton said. "And screw up the whole deal."

Dillinger grinned. "Don't worry about it," he said. "He's a front man, ain't he? Well, he'll be in front of me all the way."

"It's okay with me," Nelson said.

"And we'll use him here, too. Jack, you set up a guard watch over the old man and his wife. Twenty-four hours a day. Work it out with Carroll, Reilly, Chase and Van Meter. That will be a six-hour shift each. Homer gets first choice on the shift he wants. Give Reilly the midnight shift." He winked at them. "That stripper is not bad."

"Okay," Nelson said. "But if you get tired of her, give me the word and I'll send John Paul up to see you."

They all laughed and Dillinger stood up. "How about a little target practice?" he queried. "Getting a little rusty lately."

They had two days at Little Bohemia—two days of fresh air and bright sunshine, of long walks in the woods and target practice. And two night of poker, drinking and dancing.

Later, in his room, Pat danced for him in long, black silk stockings, the pink-tinted buds of her full breasts glowing in the semidarkness. His mind kept wandering back to Evelyn, remembering their parting words, the feel of her warm lips on his flesh. Tucson came back to him, and the night of the fire, with the two of them standing at the opened window, holding tightly to each other, her trembling fear exciting him strangely.

A lot had happened to him in the past few months. So much that he couldn't remember half of it. It seemed like a wild crazy dream when he closed his eyes and thought about it. It all seemed to whirl about in his head like the mad clanging of a merry-go-round, always the same things going around and around, over and over again. Nights, he would open his eyes and sit up in the bed to pound the sides of his head angrily.

The trouble started after dinner on Sunday night. They

were seated in the small bar next to the dining room having an after-dinner drink when the dogs began to bark.

Three customers were at the bar, talking to Emil Wanatka, unaware that the man seated in a booth against the wall was John Dillinger.

"What's the matter with the dogs?" one of the men asked. "They don't usually bark this long."

"Nothing," Emil said, nervously glancing toward Dillinger's booth. "Nothing at all."

"Sure there's something," the man said loudly. "Them dogs bark when a car goes by but they don't keep barking after it's gone."

"Excuse me," Emil said. "I've got to see Mother for a minute."

The moment Emil left the room, Dillinger jumped up. "Get him, Tommy."

Carroll looked confused. "What's that?" he said.

"Get the old man, you dumb son-of-a-bitch. The cops are out there. Kill 'em both."

The three men at the bar stood up and began edging toward the door.

"That's far enough," Dillinger said, pointing two automatics at them. He turned to Hamilton. "Where's Baby Face?"

"In his cottage with Helen and Chase."

Dillinger turned back to the three men. "Okay, you guys. Make a break for your car and don't stop for the law or I'll plug you right in the back. Now get out of here."

They looked at each other, their eyes frightened and bewildered.

"I'm Dillinger," he said. "Get it? Now get out there and run before I kill you."

They bumped into each other in their hurry to open the door. Then they ran, heedless of the voice coming to them from the darkness.

"Stop and put up your hands or we'll shoot. We're federal officers."

The men kept running. A barrage of gunfire exploded from a dozen positions in the darkness. All three men went sprawling headlong into the dirt—one dead, the other two seriously wounded.

When the shots came, Dillinger was already running across the dining room toward the stairs. Homer and Reilly ran after him. Upstairs, Hamilton was firing from an opened window of Dillinger's room. Dillinger handed them a submachine gun each and took two for himself.

"Homer, take the dining-room window. You, Reilly, get up on the roof. Let's give 'em hell for five minutes and then break for the back. Send the girls up here."

Dillinger took a window next to Hamilton and opened fire. A moment later Marie, Pat Cherrington and Jean Delaney ran breathlessly into the room.

"Get down," Hamilton warned. "On your stomachs and stay there."

"That old bastard finked on us," Dillinger said. "I sent Tommy after him."

"Never mind him," Hamilton said. "There's an army out there."

Bullets slapped against the side of the building, smashing the windows, and thudding into the wall behind them.

The sound of the two choppers in the small room was deafening. One of the girls behind him was screaming hysterically. The guns were hot in gangsters' hands and the acrid cordite smell tickled his nostrils.

Hamilton gasped and fell back, the gun clattering to the floor beside him.

"Jean, get Tommy," Dillinger shouted, and continued shooting until Carroll arrived.

"Let's drag him out of here," Dillinger said, crawling across the room toward Hamilton. "Did you get the old man?"

Carroll shook his head. "He's locked up in the cellar with his old woman."

"Why didn't you shoot the door down?"

"I couldn't. It's too thick."

Dillinger swore angrily, and began dragging Hamilton out of the room.

When the gunfire started, Baby Face Nelson was lying on the bed, listening to the news roundup on the radio.

116

"Here we go again," he said, jumping up and running to the closet for his machine gun. Helen ran after him. "You stay here," he said. "Get under the bed. John Paul, get up to the house and see what's doing."

Putting out the light inside the cabin, Nelson opened the door and stepped out into the darkness. All the action seemed to be in front of the lodge. Grinning, he ran toward it with the machine gun in his hands. Now he could see red-spitting flashes from a number of positions and, laughing maniacally, he began firing in a wide, sweeping arc.

A moment later bullets were striking the ground all around him and one whizzed so close to his ear that he felt it go by. Still grinning, he spun around and ran into the woods and disappeared.

He ran over a mile before he saw a cabin with a car parked at the side of it. Slowly, he made his way in the darkness, careful not to trip or cause any disturbing noise. He had just reached the right side of the car when he heard the sound of another car approaching. Crouching with the gun held before him, he waited silently.

The car pulled up in front of the cabin and stopped. Three men got out, then the door of the cabin opened and a man came out to greet them.

Nelson pricked up his ears.

"We're federal officers," one of the men said. "I'm Special Agent Carter Baum and this is Agent Jay Newman. And you know Mr. Christenson, the local deputy constable."

"Oh, sure. Hi, Carl. My name is Koerner. What can I do for you fellas?"

"Whose car is that?"

"It's mine."

"Fine. Can we use your phone, Mr. Koerner?"

"Sure, come in."

Suddenly, Nelson stepped out from behind the car. "I know you've got on bulletproof vests," he said. "So I'll give it to you high and low." He spoke very rapidly, the gun swinging up so that it was in position the moment he stopped talking.

"Good-bye, suckers," he said, and punched the trigger. Baum was killed instantly. Newman and Christenson fell,

117

severely wounded. Koerner jumped back into the house and slammed the door.

Nelson sent a blast through the door before leaping into the agents' car and driving off.

Carroll, Reilly and Van Meter carried Hamilton nearly two miles through the woods bordering the lake before they arrived at Ed Mitchell's Rest Lake Resort. Leading the way, Dillinger stopped before the front door and banged on it with the muzzle of the machine gun.

Attired in a nightshirt, Ed Mitchell fearfully opened the door.

Dillinger brushed past him, looking quickly about the small lobby until he found the telephone. He nodded and Carroll rushed up to the instrument and swiftly ripped it off the wall.

"Is that the only phone?" Dillinger asked.

"Yes, sir."

"We need a fast car," Dillinger said. "Whose car is that outside?"

"It belongs to Bob Johnson."

"I want it," Dillinger said. "Get me the keys."

"But—but, sir—" Ed Mitchell stammered.

"I'm Dillinger," he said. "So don't give me no trouble."

"Yes, sir." Mitchell ran outside and a moment later they could hear him knocking on a door.

"How's Jackie doing?" Dillinger asked, lighting a cigarette.

"I don't know," Homer said. "He's out cold."

"Son-of-a-bitch," he said, puffing on the butt. "I wonder what happened to Nelson."

"Chase came in during the battle," Homer said, "and ducked out again. I didn't get a chance to say a word to him."

Ed Mitchell entered the room and handed Dillinger the car keys.

"Just don't try to go nowhere," Dillinger said, walking to the door. "We've got boys all over the place. They'll kill you if you walk out."

Less than a half-hour after the attack had started at

118

Little Bohemia, all the men had escaped from the lodge. Only the owner and his wife, and the four gun molls were left behind. Nevertheless, sixteen FBI agents, armed with machine guns, automatic rifles, shotguns, tear gas equipment and steel vests, waited twelve hours before making their move. Because of the barbed-wire fences and the drainage ditch, the surrounding of the house had taken over an hour. Then, once surrounded, the agents huddled behind bushes and trees to await orders that would send them crashing headlong into a no man's land. The order did not come until dawn.

Melvin Purvis, the agent in charge of the raid, began the final stage of the attack with gas bombs.

A moment later, a small voice was heard from within the house.

"We will come out if you'll stop firing."

"Come out and bring everyone with you—with your hands up," Purvis replied.

Four women came out, followed by Emil Wanatka and his wife.

"Anybody else in there?" Purvis demanded.

They shook their heads. "We don't know," the girls said.

Purvis turned to Wanatka and his wife. It had been Wanatka who had informed the FBI of Dillinger's presence at his lodge. He had placed a note in a package of cigarettes and had given it to his brother-in-law, Herman Voss. Voss had immediately called the United States marshal in Chicago who, in turn, had called Purvis.

"I don't know, either," Emil said, holding onto his wife. "We've been in the cellar all night."

Moments later six special agents rushed the first floor of the lodge and rushed right back out again, tears streaming down their faces. Another assault group stormed the lodge. They got as far as the second floor before rushing out to put their heads under the pump. Finally, a thorough search from cellar to attic was completed.

All the government agents had to show for their night's work was four frightened but arrogant women, three automobiles, some expensive matched luggage, numerous articles

119

of clothing, machine guns, bulletproof vests, rifles, tear gas bombs, ammunition and a much-shot-up house.

The outlaws, meanwhile, had enjoyed a twelve-hour start on their getaway. The raid had been kept top secret and even that had worked to Dillinger's advantage. Once the agents left the lodge, the story of the battle spread rapidly over the countryside.

In Washington, J. Edgar Hoover had paced the floor of his office all night, waiting for reports of Dillinger's capture. Wild stories and rumors flashed across the country with the speed of sound. One story claimed that there had been a mutiny of special agents at Little Bohemia, and that Purvis and two other agents had been held in a garage at gunpoint by other special agents. Petitions were circulated demanding Purvis' removal from office. Bold headlines appeared in many newspapers: "URGE PURVIS OUSTER" "DEMAND PURVIS QUIT IN DILLINGER FIASCO." Purvis offered his resignation but Hoover refused to accept it.

The four women were taken to Madison, Wisconsin, where they were charged in federal court with harboring members of the Dillinger gang. Each of them received a probationary sentence of one year and one day. One week later they had rejoined their outlaw sweethearts.

Hamilton lay on a dirty cot in back of a saloon in Chicago for nine days without medical attention. Doc Moran had disappeared and not even Louis Piquett knew where to find him. Dillinger angrily paced the small room, shooting nervous glances at Hamilton, who appeared to be in a coma most of the time. From the position of the bullet hole, it was obvious that the slug had passed through his liver.

Now Hamilton stirred and opened his eyes. "Johnnie," he whispered. "Where's the doc?"

"He'll be here pretty soon," Dillinger said. "Just take it easy."

"How long have I been here, Johnnie?"

"Not long. A couple of days."

"It seems longer than that. I'm all mixed up. I keep

getting this crazy dream about falling down a long flight of stairs. I just tumble, head over heels, on and on, and I never reach bottom."

"It's the fever. Want some water?"

"Yeah. Is it cold?"

"Just tap. I ain't got no ice."

"I'd like some ice. I feel like I'm burning up."

"I'll get you the water."

"Put some ice in it, will ya, Johnnie? Please."

"I ain't got no ice, goddamnit," he shouted.

Hamilton turned his head and closed his eyes. "Sorry, Johnnie."

"Well, damnit, be reasonable. I'd give you some ice if I had some. I ain't got any."

"Just water, please."

Dillinger brought him a full glass and propped up his head, pouring the liquid between his parched lips. The water ran down his bearded chin and onto his soiled white shirt.

"That feels good," he said, trying to look at the wet shirt. "Pour some on my chest, Johnnie."

Dillinger emptied the glass on him and walked away.

"Thanks, Johnnie."

Dillinger whirled on him, his face contorted in anger. "Shut up, will ya? Go to sleep. What the hell do you think I am—a lousy nursemaid or something?"

Slowly, Hamilton pushed himself up to a sitting position. "Why don't you go, Johnnie? I don't need you. Get out of here while you still have a chance. I'll be okay as soon as Doc gets down here."

"Doc ain't coming," Dillinger shouted.

Hamilton's eyes narrowed. "How long have I been here, Johnnie?"

"Nine goddamn days!"

Hamilton nodded and struggled to his feet. He stood before the bed, weaving, a tall, gaunt, jaundiced-faced, heavily bearded man with sunken, black, lusterless eyes and slack mouth.

Dillinger stared at him a long time, his eyes narrowed into slits. "You okay, eh? Walk over here. Come on."

Hamilton took one staggering step and began to cough. Then another step, his legs wobbling under him, his arms stretched out for balance. And another.

Dillinger waited, his shoulders against the wall, a small smile beginning to pull at the corners of his mouth. "That's the boy, Jackie. Come on."

"Jesus, it hurts, Johnnie. I've got to stop. Help me back to the bed. Please, Johnnie. I'm dizzy. Help me."

"Come on, you yellow bastard, walk."

"Johnnie," he whispered hoarsely. "Help me, Johnnie." His arms reached out in front of him, beckoning to Dillinger. His eyelids were fluttering and two tiny streams of blood had begun to course down the sides of his mouth. "Jesus, Johnnie," he screamed. "There's something wrong inside. I can feel it. Johnnie!"

A moment later he retched loudly and blood spurted from his opened mouth. His eyes turned in his head and he sank to the floor, dead, the blood still running out of his frozen mouth.

Dillinger drove the car and Homer sat in the back with the body.

"Strip him," Dillinger said.

"Hell, Johnnie, I don't like doing that. Jack was a friend of mine."

"Don't give me no trouble," Dillinger said. "I'm in no mood for it."

"Okay, Johnnie. Anything you say."

"You sure you know where that gravel pit is?"

"Sure, Johnnie. Just about ten miles."

When they arrived at the gravel pit, Hamilton had been stripped naked. Quickly, the two men dug a shallow grave and dropped the white gleaming body into it. Timidly, Homer dropped Jack's hat on top of him.

"Nobody can identify the hat," he said. "The poor bastard has got to take something with him."

"Will you shut up?" Dillinger said, tossing him a can of lye. "Get his fingers and I'll get his face. Nobody is ever gonna identify Jackie."

"What difference would it make?"

122

"Keep the cops on their toes," he said. "They won't be so anxious to come gunning for me while they know Jack's around." He grinned and lit a cigarette. "Jack was a pretty good boy. He just never had no luck. Just no goddamn luck at all."

CHAPTER TWELVE

Now, finally, the magic was gone—in a wild fury of bullets and violence, of robbery and murder. John Dillinger, the Robin Hood of the Depression, had now become just plain "John the Killer," wanted dead or alive, but preferably dead. *Shoot to kill* was the order of the day. Enormous rewards were posted in five states and the city of Chicago.

President Roosevelt signed the Crime Bill, giving the FBI full power to go to war against the underworld. This bill allowed the attorney general of the United States to make payments up to $25,000 for information leading to the apprehension of a wanted desperado or criminal.

The newspapers, quick to scent public opinion, began screaming for Dillinger's scalp in bold, black type. The police were berated for their years of blunders; and Melvin Purvis, who had directed the FBI in a tragicomedy of errors at Little Bohemia, became the scapegoat in the face of mounting public indignation with the whole Dillinger situation.

Alone in his basement room on Dearborn Street, Dillinger read all the reports with growing apprehension and depression. Still he did not fully understand the reversal of public opinion, and he attributed the sudden change to those "goddamn" reporters who had sucked around him for stories and were now betraying him.

All the good boys were gone. Pierpont, Makley, Clark and now even Hamilton. Nelson had left for a trip to the West Coast with his wife and John Paul Chase. Eddie

Green was dead. Tommy Carroll and Pat Reilly were in hiding somewhere. Walt Dietrich was back in prison, and Joe Burns was somewhere in Chicago, also in hiding.

The only one left of the original gang was Homer Van Meter. Even Evelyn had been taken away from him. The other girls, the ones picked up in Tucson and at Little Bohemia, were out walking the streets, free as birds, while Evelyn sweated it out in a crummy cell.

He spent a week closeted in the room after Hamilton's death. Not once in all that time did he see sunlight or receive a guest except for the stooge who brought him food from the brothel's kitchen upstairs. The rent went up to $750 a week, and Ana Sage did not come down to discuss it.

At the beginning of the second week, Homer paid him a visit. He was sniffling, suffering from a bad head cold, his moist eyes swimming in pools of water.

"Where the hell have you been?" Dillinger demanded the instant he saw him.

Homer blew his nose loudly and wiped his eyes. "I've been real sick, Johnnie. Got a real bad cold."

"Well, keep away from me," Dillinger said.

"Sure, Johnnie. How have you been?"

"How do you think, holed up in this crummy hole? It's worse than solitary."

"Yeah, Marie and me got ourselves a place on Halsted. Across the street from the old place." He shook his head sadly. "Pretty lousy place."

"You got windows?"

"Yeah, sure."

"Well, it's better than this hole. Find me a place."

"This is a good place, Johnnie. Safe."

"Safe? The only way I can blast my way out of this joint is by digging out like in stir."

"Yeah, I see what you mean."

"Marie still with you?"

"Sure, I told you. She really goes for me."

Dillinger lit a cigarette and flopped on the bunk. "What's new?"

"Well, that's why I came. Louie's got a plastic surgeon

124

all lined up. Cost five grand for the job. Guaranteed to change your looks so that even your own mother wouldn't recognize you."

"How about the fingerprints?"

"That, too. You'll be like a different man."

Dillinger puffed on the cigarette a moment, squinting at the gray wall before him. "I need some dough," he said finally. "I've got a job all lined up in Fostoria, Ohio. Should be at least thirty, forty thousand."

"Who're we gonna get, Johnnie?"

"Nobody. Just you and me like the old days. We'll split it right down the middle. You still got your chopper and vest?"

"Yeah."

"Okay, get a car and we'll leave tonight at ten. Bring Marie along to drive."

"Jesus, Johnnie, I don't know. You think we should with all that heat and everything?"

Dillinger sat up quickly. "Screw the heat," he said. "You be here tonight with that dame or else."

"Okay, Johnnie, don't get mad. I'll be here."

They arrived in Fostoria early the next morning. Homer had driven all night while Dillinger had slept soundly in tht back seat. Maria had smoked and drank and napped, but had said very little to Homer who sniffed loudly and wiped his eyes and kept himself awake with a hacking cough that refused to be stopped.

At eight o'clock they had breakfast in a restaurant directly across the street from the First National Bank. Seated at a table near a large plate glass window over-looking the bank, they ate a large breakfast in a leisurely manner and spoke in low tones.

Dillinger had dyed his hair and mustache red. He wore a dark gray business suit and a light gray soft hat with a narrow brim pulled up all the way around in homburg fashion. The flashier material and cuts of earlier days had been replaced by equally expensive but less ostentatious models. The spats and patent leather shoes were also gone, and so were the fancy hand-painted ties and silk shirts.

Now he was a businessman, moderately successful and obviously conservative. The one discordant touch in the new image were the large sunglasses which he wore at all times in public, whether inside or outside, rain or shine.

He sat at the table now, the gray hat tipped to the back of his head, his fingers absently toying with his ear, his yellow eyes completely hidden by the dark lenses.

"See that janitor out there washing the window?" he said.

"Yeah," Homer said, wiping his mouth with the back of his hand.

"He came out the back way, down that alley on the south side. He's got keys to that back door and that's the way we're going in." He pushed his chair back. "You and Marie wait until I get him in the alley, then drive in after me. That way we can get the choppers in without being seen."

"That's great," Homer said, glancing happily at Marie.

"After you drop Homer," he said, touching Marie's arm. "Back out and park in front. Keep the engine running. We won't be long."

She nodded and Dillinger stood up and casually walked out of the restaurant and crossed the street.

"Hey, Pop," he said, leaning close to the old man. "I'm Dillinger. Now, you just be a good boy and take me in that bank."

"Now, see here," the janitor said, flustered, "I'm not gonna do no such thing."

Dillinger pulled out one of the automatics from under his jacket and pressed it into the old man's chest. "Any more arguing and I'll blow a hole right through you, Pop. Get going."

The old man looked at the gun gravely and began nodding his head. "Okay, young fella. It's your funeral."

They walked down the alley and stopped before the steel door while the old man fished in his pocket for the key. The car roared in behind them and Homer jumped out, holding two machine guns.

They went in through the back with the old man walking in front of them. There was still fifteen minutes before the

126

bank opened its doors to the public. Tellers were in their cages, their heads bent as they counted their money. Clerks and bank officials were already at their desks, busily shuffling through papers.

"Okay, everybody, this is a stick-up. Stay at your desks and don't push any alarm."

The alarm went off instantly. Dillinger whirled around angrily and the cartridge drum fell out of the chopper with a loud clattering noise on the marble floor. Startled, Homer started firing wildly into the tellers' cages. One teller screamed and went down, another one reeled back, clutching his shoulder.

Dillinger swore at Homer, struggling to get the drum back into the chopper. "Get the goddamn money, you dumb son-of-a-bitch," he screamed, racing across the lobby and leaping over the guard rail.

The old janitor ran out the back door, yelling for the police. Two bank guards came rushing out of an office and nearly collided with Dillinger, who fired point blank at them. Both guards went toppling back into the office, pained and startled expressions on their white faces. People were running in all directions.

"Freeze, everybody!" Dillinger shouted. "Freeze or I'll kill you." He punched the trigger, turning everybody into pillars of salt.

"That's better," he said, looking nervously about him. Homer had disappeared into the opened vault.

There was a loud tapping on the front door and the sound of excited voices. Dillinger looked but couldn't see anything through the drawn shade. Moments later, Homer came running out of the vault with the bag of money in his hand.

"Did you get it all?" Dillinger shouted.

"Just about."

"Get it all. Go on, shake it up."

"But, Johnnie—"

"Get it!"

Two minutes later, Homer came out again and Dillinger ran to the front door and stopped three feet away from it. "You guys clear out of here," he shouted. Then, raising the chopper, he fired through the door, high enough to miss anyone standing behind it.

When they came out the street and sidewalks were empty. White-faced, Marie waited behind the steering wheel. As they drove away, people ran out of alleys and stores and pointed at the disappearing car until it was gone. The robbery had netted them barely seventeen thousand dollars. Five persons were wounded, none mortally. It was the biggest fiasco in Dillinger's career, and the last one.

One week later, in the home of James Probasco, Dillinger underwent plastic surgery, performed by Dr. Wilhelm Loeser, a dope pusher and ex-inmate of Leavenworth Penitentiary. A mole was plucked from his forehead, between his eyes, the cleft in his chin was removed, two slices were taken from his cheeks near the ears, and some minor alteration was done to his nose. In an attempt to change his fingerprints, an operation was performed on the points of the core and the delta.

With his hair and mustache now dyed black, and gold-rimmed spectacles replacing the sunglasses, Dillinger walked out of Probasco's house two weeks later. In his pockets were papers identifying him as Frank Sullivan, an employee of the Board of Trade.

At first he had been disappointed in the operation. But after days of staring into the mirror, he gradually became awart of the subtle changes and began to appreciate them. If anything, it improved his looks, making him appear younger.

Homer and Marie drove him back to the Dearborn Street hideout and waited in the car while he went down to collect his belongings. They had found a new place for him on Halsted.

While he was packing, Ana Sage rushed in, pulling a statuesque blonde in after her. "She's been simply dying to meet you," Ana said. "Her name is Polly Hamilton. Good girl."

Polly Hamilton did not immediately impress Dillinger.

The name Hamilton, he liked. It had been lucky for him in the past, maybe it could be again.

Polly was absolutely stunned at the sight of the famous desperado. "Golly," said Polly. "You're real cute."

Dillinger removed the gold-rimmed spectacles and thoughtfully rubbed his chin. "You're not bad yourself, sister."

Polly giggled and rolled her great big blue eyes. Her golden hair fell in shining ringlets about her head. "I could go for you," she said.

"You've got to move pretty fast to go with me," he said.

"You'd be surprised." She shifted her right leg, pushing out a well-rounded hip. "I'm built for wear, honey." She pressed her hands against the bodice of her dress, pulling the material tight across the nipples of her full breasts.

"That's a two-buck line," Dillinger said, returning to his packing.

"Now, Johnnie," Ana said. "She's young and new at the business. Why, hell, she's almost a virgin."

"What's that?" he asked, still packing.

"Well, you know. The kid is hardly broken in. She's still full of juice and pep."

"And you're full of crap," he said.

"Johnnie, I'm telling you. This girl is simply mad about you. She's been talking about you for months. Frankly, I think she was jealous of Evelyn."

"I still am," Polly said. "She's in jail and I'm here and you still don't care about nobody but her."

Dillinger stopped and turned to face Ana. "What's the pitch?"

"Nothing. Just trying to give you a break."

"Oh? I thought she was getting the break."

"It's a break for both of you, believe me."

"I'll think about it," Dillinger said. "Now get out of here and let me finish packing."

CHAPTER THIRTEEN

The room on Halsted had two windows, both of which looked down into a squalid alley of garbage cans and ancient rubble. Directly across and on both sides were the bleak walls of tenement buildings. The only way he could see the sky was to stick his head out the window and look straight up. It had been decades since a ray of sunlight had entered that room.

Dillinger spent the days sleeping and the nights walking the streets of Chicago. One night while in the vicinity of Ana's brothel, he stopped in and took Polly to a movie. Afterwards she returned to his room with him and spent the night. A few days later, he called her up and took her to another movie. Again she spent the night. The third time he took her to a movie, Ana went along with them.

July was a real sizzler that year. Dillinger stripped down to white shirt and slacks. The shoulder holsters and big automatics were left behind in the room when he went out in the evenings. His only weapon was a snub-nosed .38 automatic which he carried in a back pocket of his gray flannel trousers. He wore a sailor straw at a rakish angle and smoked cigars almost exclusively.

Never a day went by without his name appearing on the front page of every Chicago newspaper. Even bank robberies committed as far away as California were attributed to him. Reading about his presence in all those various places gave him a strange detached feeling. It was as if he were reading about a ghost, someone he had known, but who was now dead, and the newspapers were trying to blow life back into him with millions of empty, meaningless words.

He thought about new bank jobs. Of picking up a new gang of good boys, starting out all over again. But it

130

would take time. The heat was too great now. He would have to wait for things to cool down. Wait until the time was ripe again like it had been just a year ago when he had blazed his name across the Midwest.

People had been proud to know him then—guys in service stations, stores, hotels and restaurants. Guys everywhere had spotted him and winked conspiratorially as if the whole thing were one big game.

"Good luck, Johnnie," some had whispered, tugging on his coat sleeve. "Give 'em hell."

All the glitter had turned to grit. Why it had happened that way, he didn't know. He didn't know why it had happened the other way, either. He had started out to rob banks. Nothing else. The fame had surprised and confused him more than anybody else.

Evelyn had said it was because he was good-looking and the women had a crush on him. Piquett had said it was because of the Depression. Some reporters had blamed his harsh treatment from the law, saying that people sympathized with him. Whatever the reason or reasons, it had gone as fast as it had come.

By the middle of July he was desperate for money. Homer loaned him a couple of hundred dollars on the promise that they would get back to work in a few days. All he had to do was round up a few good boys. He telephoned Piquett and told him he wanted to get in touch with some of the boys—Joe Burns, Tommy Carroll, Baby Face Nelson, Pat Reilly, even John Paul Chase.

Then the bad news came back to him via Piquett and the grapevine. Tommy Carroll was dead, shot down by the cops in Waterloo, Iowa. Pat Reilly was in jail. Baby Face Nelson was still on the West Coast with John Paul Chase. Joe Burns was around but refused to have any dealings with Dillinger.

Piquett finally advised Dillinger to lie low for at least another month. The FBI was questioning everybody who had ever known him, tracing all their movements for the past fourteen months. Piquett, himself, had been questioned seven times. They had even offered him a slice of the reward money. But, of course, he had turned it down. Dillinger was

131

his friend, but he didn't know if he could say the same for other people. Dillinger would be very wise to watch his steps. By all means, stay away from old contacts.

On Saturday afternoon, July 22, 1934, Dillinger called Polly and invited her to a movie.

"What movie?" she asked.

"I don't know yet. Either the Marbro or the Biograph. I'll let you know later."

"Oh, Johnnie, is it okay if Ana comes? She never gets a chance to go out and she does enjoy your company."

"Sure. I'll pick you up around eight."

He took a nap after talking to Polly and slept till seven. Then he took a cold bath, shaved and put on a fresh pair of gray flannel slacks and a clean white shirt. He wiped his straw hat with a damp cloth and touched up his white shoes.

Lighting a cigar, he went out and hailed a cab. Polly was on the sidewalk in front of her place waiting for him when he arrived.

"Where's Ana?" he asked, stepping out of the cab.

"She's still fussing," Polly laughed. "Got herself a new red dress the other day and she's wearing it for the first time tonight."

"Well, tell her to shake it up. The picture starts at eight-thirty."

"What are we gonna see?"

"*Manhattan Melodrama* with Clark Gable, William Powell and Myrna Loy."

"Oh, golly," she said. "That's at the Biograph way up on the North Side. I'd better get her." She ran up the stone steps and Dillinger leaned against the cab, puffing contentedly on the cigar.

It was nearly eight-fifty when they entered the Biograph. The main feature had just started. It was the story of two lifelong friends orphaned by a river-steamer fire. One became governor of the state and the other a gangster and murderer. The gangster's girl marries the governor, and the gangster, in a grand gesture, rejects the governor's pardon and goes to the chair. It was a heartbreaking story and Polly cried profusely. Ana seemed more nervous than impressed.

"Sucker," Dillinger said as they stood up to leave. "I would have taken the pardon, then showed that bastard what was what."

"Golly, I just love Clark Gable," Polly said, dabbing her eyes with a little handkerchief. "Ain't he just the best actor ever? That was so sad. I don't like sad endings. Do you?"

Dillinger shrugged. "I had that guy figured all wrong. I never thought he was going to cop out like that."

They came out into the lobby and Dillinger placed the straw hat on the back of his head and stopped to light a fresh cigar. People crowded around them, pushing toward the sidewalk. The two women walked beside him, one on each side.

"How about something to eat?" he said, as they reached the sidewalk and turned north on Lincoln Avenue.

"I'm starved," Polly said. "I just feel empty inside."

Dillinger turned to Ana who had moved nearly an arm's length away. "Hey," he said, "where you—?"

Then he heard the voice behind him. A thin, trembling voice calling out to him. "Stick 'em up, Johnnie. We have you surrounded!"

For a split second that seemed to drag into eternity, his heart stopped beating and his mind went totally blank. He stood there on the sidewalk, arrested in motion like a wax statue. Then suddenly his heart was beating again, loud and hard, rapping against his rib cage as if the wild surge of blood had dislodged it and it was now floating free in the empty cavern of his chest. His throat constricted and he could taste the acrid bite of fear in his mouth.

Instinctively, like a trapped animal, he sensed his doom. And like a trapped animal, he reacted to the panic in the only way he knew.

He crouched, his eyes glinting, his hand darting for the gun in his back pocket, his body weaving as he began to move forward.

All motion seemed suspended in time. He heard Polly's

133

fearful shriek. He saw Ana slink away, her hard face white, her black eyes devouring him in their unblinking intensity.

Men with guns were running at him from all sides, their tensed faces inscrutable. He felt his foot slowly rise from the pavement, his hand arcing back endlessly for the gun, his body bending at the hips, his head floating down toward the pavement. And there, on the pavement, he saw the yellow stain at the tip of a cigarette butt, two broken matches, a blue ticket stub. It was all so clear and sharp, and yet so unreal, so weird, so frightening.

The explosion was deafening. The slug smashed into his back and came out through his chest, making a small hole through the white shirt. He looked down and saw the blood spurt through the hole. His mouth opened in protest and he tried to raise his arms in surrender.

There was another explosion, and another slug thudded into his back, again coming out his chest, making another small hole in his white shirt, right under his heart. Fearfully, he slapped both hands against the holes and slowly sank to his knees.

He was still conscious but he couldn't feel the hot, searing pain any more. The third slug dug into the back of his neck and came out just under his right eye. He toppled over and rolled on his back, the blood running down his face, into his opened mouth.

A film glazed his eyes as he stared up at the faces bending over him. A man was saying something to him, his lips moving quickly, nervously. There was a gun in the man's hand and it was aimed straight at his head.

A crowd had gathered and they were all staring at him. One man was grinning and his teeth were bent and crooked between his wet lips.

The man above him was still talking, trying to push people away. Then the man reached down and loosened the belt on his trousers. He tried to object but his whole body was paralyzed. He couldn't feel or hear anything.

The crowd was moving closer now and suddenly a woman broke through the line of policemen and dropped before him, quickly dipping her handkerchief in his blood. He

134

closed his eyes. There were others breaking through the line now and he opened his eyes to see two women dipping pieces of newspaper in his blood. *God*, he thought, *I must be losing a lot of blood*. He closed his eyes again.

A moment later, John Dillinger was dead.

The End

EPILOGUE

Dillinger's violent death added the crowning touch to the Dillinger legend. Like Jesse James and other legendary hero-villians, he was betrayed by someone he trusted.

Ana Sage (real name Ana Cumpanas), who earned her living in the flesh markets of Gary, Indiana and Chicago's Dearborn Street, sold out Dillinger to the FBI for $5,000 and the promise of a kindly word to the Immigration and Naturalization Service people who wanted to deport her back to her native Rumania as an undesirable alien. She collected the $5,000 but was deported a few months later. She died in a small town near Bucharest.

Homer Van Meter was the first to go after Dillinger's death. He was slain by police officials in St. Paul on August 22, 1934, while resisting arrest.

Charles Makley, who had been sentenced to die in the electric chair on October 22, 1934, was killed while attempting to escape from the Ohio prison on September 22, 1934. Harry Pierpont was executed as scheduled.

Baby Face Nelson was next in line. The death of Dillinger threw Nelson into a panic. G-man heat was everywhere. He kept on the move for four months, driving nights, sleeping in the back of the car and in dingy motels during the day, sending John Paul Chase and his wife, Helen, into small towns to buy groceries, while he waited in the woods, hugging a machine gun to his chest.

Then, late on the afternoon of November 27, 1934, while driving toward Chicago, Nelson spotted a sedan with two special agents in it, going East.

"I don't like the way those guys looked at me," Nelson said, giving chase. "Let 'em have it."

John Paul Chase, seated in the back with an automatic

137

rifle across his lap, quickly went into action. "I'll get 'em," he cried, firing through the windshield.

The special agents returned the fire. Bullets pounded into the back of their car, puncturing the gas tank. They pulled the car off into a side road, jumped out and made ready to do battle when the desperadoes came by.

They never did. Instead they turned down another road and found themselves being chased by another police car, manned by Special Agent Ed Hollis and Inspector Sam Cowley, who had supervised the capture of Dillinger.

Baby Face brought the car to a squealing stop and leaped out with Chase at his side. By the time Hollis and Cowley had brought their own car to a stop and jumped out, Nelson was waiting for them with a chopper and Chase with the automatic rifle.

Without hesitation Nelson emptied the gun at the two agents. Hollis had time to fire one blast from his shotgun before Nelson's bullets cut him down. Nelson fell back, clutching his stomach, disappearing behind the car. Chase and Cowley continued to exchange fire. Helen Gillis lay cowering in a ditch.

Then in a last desperate sally, Nelson staggered out into the open, firing as he advanced toward Cowley who was already on the ground, mortally wounded. Nelson stumbled into the government car and, with his wife and Chase, drove off. Nelson died that night. His body was found the next morning, nude and blood-splattered, beside a cemetery wall.

John Probasco, who had harbored Dillinger, took his life by leaping from the nineteenth-floor window of the FBI bureau office in Chicago.

Doc Moran was last seen cutting across Lake Erie in a motorboat. Underworld rumor is that he won't be showing up for a long time.

Dr. Wilhelm Loeser was sentenced to serve one day for the face-lifting operation and returned to complete a three-year sentence on a narcotics charge he had been previously paroled on.

Joe Burns was captured in Chicago on December 17, 1934, and returned to Indiana State Prison.

Pat Cherrington was sentenced to serve two years, Opal Long six months, Helen Gillis one year, Marie Conforti one year, Jean Delaney one year, all for harboring Dillinger or members of his gang.

Louis Piquett was sentenced to two years at Leavenworth Penitentiary and fined $10,000.

Dr. Clayton E. May, who treated Dillinger's leg wound in Minneapolis, was sentenced to two years and fined $1,000 for failing to report it.

John Paul Chase was apprehended in California and sentenced to a life term at Alcatraz. There, a year later, he met Eddie Bentz who, when captured by special agents, expressed the hope he'd be sent to Alcatraz. Surprised, the agents sought the reason for such an unusual request. Bentz frowned slightly. "Why, gentlemen," he said. "All my friends are there."

On her release from prison, Evelyn Frechette toured the country as the chief attraction of a carnival side show. She told wide-eyed audiences of her life with Johnnie Dillinger. "He liked to dance and he liked to hunt," she said, pausing, her eyes twinkling across the gaping faces. "He—excuse me if you've heard this one—was a pretty good shot. He loved music but very seldom sang. But when he did sing, his favorites were, *Happy Days Are Here Again* and *The Last Roundup*."

The death of Dillinger marked the end of one of the strangest epochs in American criminal history. He was, in a way, a phenomenon, as strange as the Depression itself.

John Dillinger was many things to many people, but whether he ever understood what he was to himself is doubtful. There have been thousands of criminals, desperadoes, bandits, hoodlums and gangsters. But only one Jesse James and one John Dillinger. Separated by much more history than years, they were, nevertheless, brothers under the skin. Though ruthless and violent men, they had that touch of magic that somehow transcends evil.

THE END